D0096345

More Advance Praise for *Kids, Parents & Money*

"A practical, helpful, usable, and useful book providing both parent and child a broad overview of family and life finances. A wonderful hands-on book with real world application."

—Richard Baker, Chairman
Baker Book House Co.

"Never have I seen a better primer to have kids interact with their parents on one of the most essential and neglected issues in life. I wish I had it earlier. But obviously one can always start anytime, and there is nothing like the present moment. Why be vague about money—know what's in your checkbook, know what you can afford, and have a savings plan. It's a work in progress, one step at a time!"

—Pat Boyle, Attorney at Law
Chicago, Illinois

KIDS,
PARENTS
& MONEY

KIDS, PARENTS & MONEY

Teaching Personal Finance from Piggy Bank to Prom

WILLARD S. STAWSKI II

John Wiley & Sons, Inc.

New York • Chichester • Weinheim • Brisbane • Singapore • Toronto

This book is printed on acid-free paper. ∞

Copyright © 2000 by Williard S. Stawski II. All rights reserved.

Published by John Wiley & Sons, Inc.

Published simultaneously in Canada.

No part of this publication may be reproduced, stored in a retrieval system or transmitted in any form or by any means, electronic, mechanical, photocopying, recording, scanning or otherwise, except as permitted under Section 107 or 108 of the 1976 United States Copyright Act, without either the prior written permission of the Publisher or authorization through payment of the appropriate per-copy fee to the Copyright Clearance Center, 222 Rosewood Drive, Danvers, MA 01923, (978) 750-8400, fax (978) 750-4744. Requests to the Publisher for permission should be addressed to the Permissions Department, John Wiley & Sons, Inc., 605 Third Avenue, New York, NY 10158-0012, (212) 850-6011, fax (212) 850-6008, E-Mail: PERMREQ@WILEY.COM.

This publication is designed to provide accurate and authoritative information in regard to the subject matter covered. It is sold with the understanding that the publisher is not engaged in rendering professional services. If professional advice or other expert assistance is required, the services of a competent professional person should be sought.

ISBN: 0-471-35947-5

Printed in the United States of America

10 9 8 7 6 5 4 3 2 1

To my main men:
Jordan, Jacob, Preston, Justin,
and Sam Stawski

Contents

Step 2

SET YOUR OBJECTIVES   69

Step 3

LOOK FOR OPPORTUNITY   99

Step 4

BE AWARE OF YOUR EMOTIONS   135

Step 5

SAVING AND PERSONAL
RECORD KEEPING   159

Step 6
GOAL ATTAINMENT 227

Step 7
ATTAIN AGAIN 239

Acknowledgments

THIS WORK CAME TOGETHER AS A RESULT OF MANY YEARS OF growth, development, and experience as a husband, father, and financial consultant. Most practical applications found in this work are a result of parental trial and error. Fortunately, our kids Jordan, Justin, Jacob, Preston, and Sam aren't too messed up as a result of the experience. I don't know if the same can be said of my wife, Lisa, and me.

Speaking of Lisa, through her efforts above and beyond the call of duty, she has made my parental journey significantly less stressful than it could have been.

The example set by my parents, David and Barb, were drawn from on numerous occasions throughout the writing of this book. Thanks, guys. Their mothers (my grandmothers), Donna Stawski and Harriet Bowens, can take the credit for many of the "old-style values" exemplified herein.

Moral and business support from my very dear friend Michael Bonadio enabled me to work the many long, lonely hours pounding this book out. This support was much needed because of my relatively inefficient three-finger typing method. Thanks for being there.

Many thanks to our very dear friends Scott and Amy Shurlow. It is because of their friendship, support, and vacation properties that our family has maintained at least a small degree of sanity through an otherwise stressful entrepreneurial experience.

Tom, Jeffery, and Myron Molotky have been great friends and marvelous professional associates. Their support has been tremendous and their business acumen unmatched. We're lucky to know you.

Way-to-go and thanks for noticing our booth at Book Expo 1998 to Debby Englander and company at John Wiley & Sons. Your editorial skills, and the input from Michael Detweiler, make me look and sound better than I am.

Thanks to Gary Nash, Bob Eleveld, Doug Kool, Jim Hovinga, Dan Van Timmeren, Bill Cutler, and Jerry Van Woerkom. I appreciate your support more than you will ever know.

I greatly appreciate the support and feedback of many of the thousands of Cash University families that have been using the system. Their success and correspondence reassured us that we were on the right track in providing a valuable financial learning tool.

I must acknowledge the many teachers, authors, and mentors I have had over the years. Their combined influence has made it possible for me to accomplish this work and keep it interesting for the reader.

The Internet earned high honors as this masterpiece was assembled. Countless are the hours and incalculable the dollars saved by bringing the world to me instead of me to it. The Internet truly is this generation's greatest opportunity and benefit.

And, finally, I must express my thanks for the benefit of peace and contentment derived through the Higher Power in my life.

Introduction

As I sat in my Cash University display booth at BookExpo 1998, I noticed a group of well-dressed individuals headed my way. As they reached our small booth, they stopped and entered. I looked at their name tags and discovered it was a group from the publishing firm John Wiley & Sons. After some initial chitchat, one of the group mentioned they really thought our concept was unique and asked if I had ever thought about writing a book on our system. Quite frankly, I had not, but the idea was intriguing. Throughout the course of their visit, we exchanged business cards and some light ideas and they departed.

Over the next several months a contract was drawn up and the deal was sealed. "Okay," I thought, "now what?" I had written some excellent letters in my day and a couple of good business plans, but a book? With my experience in the brokerage business and having developed an extensive database on children and money, I figured I was probably the right person for the job. Children's financial literacy is an excellent topic, and every parent needs to learn about teaching it. If anyone is gong to write an effective hands-on guide to teaching children financial skills, it's going to be me.

The more I thought about it, the more I realized that the information we had compiled over the years would be terrific content for a book. Likewise, I realized that the need for this specialized information is getting greater every day. The Cash University system was designed to provide the most basic lessons in financial and family skills to young children and their parents. Kids and parents work together to create an environment of learning and growth in the home. If you look at the news, you'll discover that the need for this kind of interaction grows daily. While this book is largely about teaching children financial principles, it's also about family relationships. You can't have one without the other.

One thing we've grown to realize throughout the development of Cash University is that grandparents identify very clearly with why financial literacy is important. Why is this? We believe it's because they have "been there" and "done that." Grandparents are living examples of why financial literacy is important to learn and understand as a child. Consider this question: If today's grand-parents were nurtured in the same manner, generally speaking, as children are today, would they have had the discipline and knowl-edge necessary to attain the financial security they now enjoy? I think we all know the answer to the question and henceforth see clearly why it's important to take an active role in teaching our children financial and life skills.

Our children have a significant advantage over their parents and grandparents. Opportunity exists today that would have been science fiction only a decade earlier. This advantage will not, how-ever, compensate for a lack of planning and knowledge. In order for our children to fully enjoy the opportunities that will become available to them, they need to first understand the financial fundamentals, like their grandparents did. Once our children are equipped with basic financial intelligence and a sense of purpose, only then will they be able to take full advantage of the opportu-nities that await them.

We see it daily in the parents we talk to, opportunity lost because of previous financial mismanagement. An individual's credit history will follow them everywhere and it will affect everything in their lives. We've seen parents that have missed out on great chances because of substandard credit ratings. Families are falling apart because parents haven't been able to handle self-inflicted financial pressures. Children are being raised by babysitters and teachers because both parents are drawn from the home to create enough income to pay massive, want-based bills. Families lose their focus because personal material "wants" are selfishly recategorized to "needs." A bigger house, a better car, and nicer clothes—what does all this mean when you are eighty-five and you haven't seen your kids or grandkids in six months?

This book is about priorities as much as it is about finance. If you put your priorities in the right place, you'll reap benefits far greater than financial success; you'll achieve life success. Your children are blank pieces of canvas that everybody gets to draw on. Their friends draw on them, their babysitters draw on them, their teachers and coaches draw on them, the media draw on them, and their family members draw on them. The resulting life image will depend on who has spent the most time at the easel.

What do the images look like today? Is it evident who is spending the most time drawing? Can you tell who the predominant artist is when you or anyone else looks at the canvas? My wife and I are always learning to be better artists. Through the challenges we have raising our five boys, as well as the experiences running Cash University, we learn new and improved drawing techniques daily.

I hope this book benefits you and your family. I've had a terrific time writing it and hope that you have the same reading it. There is ample opportunity for you to implement new drawing techniques through the "Chapter Challenges" at the close of each chapter. These activities are simple financial- and communications-based ideas for you and your family members.

If you ask anybody that is happy and over sixty-five years old where a person's priorities should be, I'll bet the answers will be similar. Learn their family-centered lesson while you're young, and then live life to its fullest for you and your children. Take the time to talk with your kids and let them know how important they are to you. Once you've established a basic level of communication and trust, they'll be receptive to anything you say. Remember, you are their favorite artist.

OVERVIEW

OUR CHILDREN

···

CHAPTER 1

How Do You Want Your Kids to Turn Out?

Do not teach your children, for they will not understand.
Rather, show them how you live and they will follow you. . . .

—JACQUELINE WATTS

ALL OF US HAVE GONE THROUGH THE SAME EXPERIENCES IN OUR lives, relatively speaking. We've been born, come home from the hospital, pooped in our pants, gotten cleaned up by a parent who cared about us, learned to walk and talk, learned to be nice, learned to beg, learned to _____ (go ahead and fill in the blank for a behavior of your choice). The fact is, virtually everything we've ever done has been a result of a learned behavior. The way we react to others, the way we decide things, the way we spend and save money, the way we choose to earn a living: All of these thoughts and actions are a result, to some degree, of behavior that we have learned.

With this in mind, it is clear that our parents had a great deal to do with how we turned out. Some of us had great parents who spent a lot of time with us and showed us how to be effective in our lives and with others. Some of us—the larger percentage, unfortunately—had parents who may not have spent enough time and energy on our behalf. Consequently, we may lack some of the life and parenting skills necessary to live and parent effectively. Some of us had two parents, some of us had one parent, and some of us had no parents. Whatever the case may be, whoever was there for us when we grew up was the one responsible for our early development. How we decide to do things today is a reflection on the values and habits promoted by those parental influences.

Now, let's spin things forward a few years and look at ourselves and our own children. Let's look at how much time we spend teaching our kids how to do cool things. Let's look at the example we set and at the level of communication present in our family relationships. Let's look at the financial example we are setting through our own spending and saving habits. Whatever we do and say is what our children will be learning to apply to their own lives. What they learn today is what they'll implement tomorrow.

When our kids go out and buy this book in a few years and reflect back on their family experiences, what kinds of memories do you think they'll have? What kinds of family and financial habits will they have adopted? What family and financial principles will they be implementing in their own lives and families at the time? I hope that after implementing some of the ideas in this book and spending some quality time with your kids, they'll look back happily on a positive, fulfilling childhood experience and see what role that experience played in the development of their financially and emotionally rewarding adult life experience.

The purpose of this book is to help you work with your family to establish some basic communication skills and to create an environment in your home that is peaceful, challenging, happy, positive, and rewarding. You and your children will also gain substantial financial intelligence through the contents and processes of this work.

Chapter Challenge ....

Purchase a one-inch three-ring binder that has a clear plastic cover to insert a cover page. From now on, this will become your family journal. Also pick up a three-hole punch, lined paper, and copy paper. If you have access to the Internet, visit www.kidsparentsandmoney.com and bookmark it. From this point forward, we'll refer to www.kidsparentsandmoney.com as "KPM.com." Once on the site, print out a Cover Sheet and Form CC-1, complete the Cover Sheet, and insert it into the front of your new binder. Complete Form CC-1, punch holes in the form, and place it at the beginning of your journal. If you don't have the Internet, on the first page, write down the date and document three things you have done recently to positively affect the lives of your children. Also, write down your reasons for purchasing this book and any thoughts you may have on your family relationships as they now stand.

....

CHAPTER 2

State of the Union

In challenging times, when ethics are more important
than ever before, make sure you set a good example
for everyone you work and live with.

—RALPH WALDO EMERSON

WHEN I WAS GROWING UP, I DON'T RECALL MUCH MEDIA attention focused on the economy. I grew up in the 1960s and 1970s, and I don't remember a lot of talk about bankruptcy. There didn't seem to be a lot of talk about credit card debt, and there certainly wasn't any talk about any kind of massive national debt. I remember hearing about Vietnam and Watergate. I fuzzily recall the Cold War but clearly remember *Gilligan's Island, The Partridge Family,* and *The Brady Bunch.*

Today, however, times are quite different. Kids today are keenly aware of what's happening in the world. They are much more informed and concerned than we ever were. They have the Internet and 124 channels of cable to view. As a result of all these information sources, we need to be more involved in our children's lives than our parents ever were in ours. Because of rapidly changing technology, there are more forces that affect the lives of our children than we ever dreamed of when we were their age. We've got to be there for our children.

When we choose to play an active role in our children's life education, we alter the course for generations to come. If our children learn effective life and financial skills from us, chances are that they will teach our grandchildren these same lessons. If we choose not to prepare our children effectively, our grandchildren will suffer the greater consequence. Consider this fact. Recent demographic statistics are essentially the result of nurturing that took place twenty to thirty years ago. The effect our parents had on us is readily apparent in the numbers we see. As you consider the following statistics, consider the likely situation in thirty years if the course is left unaltered.

In 1998 there were a record 1.3 million personal bankruptcies in the United States; this number is projected to rise to 1.35 million in 1999. In 1994 *nonmortgage consumer debt* was $902 billion. In 1996 that number grew to $1.16 *trillion,* and in 1997 it was $1.216 *trillion.* This number is much more impressive when you write it out: $1,216,000,000,000. According to the Bureau of Public Debt, the *outstanding public debt* as of December 20, 1999 at 4:18:32 P.M. PST was $5,705,071,498,034.02. This means that every citizen of the United States has a share equal to $20,801.12. The national debt has continued to increase at an average of $257 million per day since December 31, 1998. To check where we are each day, visit KPM.com and check the debt clock. Most of this debt was incurred over the last twenty years, a period of unparalleled economic growth and prosperity! Figure 2-1 shows how personal debt has risen over the years.

In 1997 the Jump$tart Coalition for Personal Financial Literacy conducted a study of 1,532 high school seniors from sixty-five schools across the country. The purpose of the study was to determine the overall level of financial literacy among students and gauge whether young adults have what it takes to make it on their own. The survey covered basic questions in subjects such as insurance, credit, borrowing, earning, and saving. Results of the survey showed that only 10.2% of students were able to score higher

FIGURE 2-1   Outstanding Public Debt

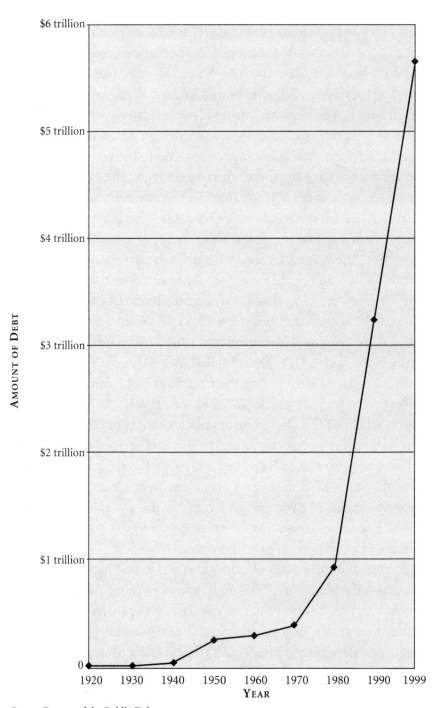

Source: Bureau of the Public Debt

than 75%. In fact, the average score was just 57.3%, a failing grade in any school district.

Another interesting result of the survey was a *negative* relationship between student scores and the personal bankruptcy rates in their states. What this means is that the lower the level of financial literacy, the higher the likelihood of personal bankruptcy on a state-by-state basis. This only makes sense; if you don't understand how money works, you're not likely to manage it properly.

The survey shows that our kids are going out into the world without the necessary financial skills to survive. Credit cards are easier to obtain than ever before. There is no social opposition to financial mismanagement, and bankruptcy appears to be an acceptable solution to financial problems.

Considering this situation, it's not surprising that a recent study by the Marist Institute for Public Opinion concluded that 28% of individuals surveyed said they always worry that their bills will go unpaid; 33% said they sometimes worry; 22% said they seldom worry; and only 17% said they never worry. If these survey respondents are parents, what example are they setting for their children, and what financial habits are those children developing?

Today, many adults suffer from financial rudderlessness. In other words, they have no direction regarding how they spend their money. They live, charge, pay bills, get stressed out, hope for a raise, and then spend more. Their personal cash flow is their thrust, but they have no rudder to create directed travel.

In order to create a home environment that is conducive to family happiness and financial health, we must become conscious of personal financial illiteracy and take steps to protect our family members from it. We can begin this process by taking steps to change our behavior first. Only after we've made the determination to be a better example can we work effectively with our children.

Throughout this book, I'll offer numerous suggestions that will help you make necessary changes in your finances. Personal change can be almost instantaneous. If you decide to eliminate personal debt, you'll be able to effect an immediate change. Resolve to pay off your credit cards and personal loans, establish a family emergency cash account, and then start paying off your cars and your home. Through this simple process, you can free yourself from financial bondage and experience the rush of personal liberation. Once you experience this freedom, you'll never return to financial rudderlessness and your children will be financially literate enough to never have to experience the malady for themselves. By reading this book you'll learn a lifestyle pattern that, once implemented, will make a substantial difference in your financial attitude, literacy, and habits.

Chapter Challenge ....

Become aware of your personal financial situation. Access the Internet and go to KPM.com. Print out Form CC-2 and complete it. If you don't have the Internet, list in your journal all of your debts and arrange them in order of size. Select your smallest debt, set a date by which the debt will be gone, and create a plan to eliminate that obligation within the next sixty days. Become aware of the effect your debt has on your life. Make your indebtedness a tangible circumstance and comprehend the magnitude of debt in your life. Write your thoughts and impressions in your journal. Once you become aware of the significance of debt in your life, you'll want to eliminate it as soon as possible. This book with its supporting Internet site will help you do so. As you make a personal commitment to eliminate your debt, the example you set for your children will do more to enhance their financial acuity than any book you can read. If you provide the right example and teach your children well, you can be assured that you have done your best at helping them avoid the hazards of financial mismanagement.

....

CHAPTER 3

Who's Teaching Financial Literacy Anyway?

Winners make decisions based on the future they desire, while losers make decisions based on the present they desire.

—Anonymous

Where did you learn your money skills? Was it in college? Was it in high school? Junior high? How about in Elementary School? If you're like me, none of the above is the response. Most people learn about money only through trial and error. No formal course teaches the basics of personal finance.

Think about the following: Joe's family loved and cared for him. He graduated near the top of his class and attended a prominent university where he excelled further. Again he graduated near the top of his high school class and was accepted to an excellent graduate school. After spending another two years working on his MBA, he graduated and got a job with a Fortune 500 company. In his new job, Joe worked harder than most of his peers and was promoted rapidly ahead of them. Joe's income skyrocketed, and by age thirty-two, he was earning more than $125,000 a year.

Unfortunately, when his company downsized and he lost his job, Joe had to declare bankruptcy because of his tremendous personal indebtedness. All his accomplishments were diminished by his financial mismanagement.

This story serves to illustrate the importance of financial literacy. You can spend a great amount of energy and resources to obtain a substantial income, but if you don't take care of your finances, the other successes will never matter.

So where do people learn financial skills? According to the Jump$tart survey mentioned earlier, 10.9% learned about money management at school, 58.5% learned at home, and 26.4% said they learned by experience. With schools offering little in the way of a formal money management curriculum and experience being the politically correct way of saying "hard knocks," it appears that by far the greatest amount of effective financial education comes from the home. However, only homes in which a positive financial example is set and where the money can flow freely to support an effective financial lesson serve as positive role models.

Who is teaching the lessons? I don't know of many financial tutors visiting homes, so the answer must be us, the parents. We are teaching our children whatever they know about money management mostly by our example. Without any structured "lesson plan," we are leaving personal financial education largely to chance. We, as parents, may just be hoping that our kids will pick up some good money skills before they leave home.

Since you're reading this book, you've already demonstrated a desire to do more than just leave your children's financial education to chance. You've probably set forth in your mind an objective to be more than just a good financial example. You want to impact your children's financial intelligence in a way that will be meaningful and lasting. You've realized that by implementing a structured plan to teach your kids basic life and financial skills, you position them to make the most out of their lives. By diligently working with your children through their important formative years, you can protect them from the pitfalls of financial illiteracy for a lifetime.

By implementing a simple lesson plan in your home and setting a good example, you will do more for your children's success than any educational institution ever could. Before you can teach financial literacy, however, you've got to be the example. You've got to have your own financial intelligence first, so that your children can do as you do, not just as you say.

Before I address teaching your children financial skills, I will first use a few chapters to talk about your family. We need to discuss what you can do to create an environment that is conducive to the financial lessons I have prepared for you.

In my family, we've found that communication, positive reinforcement, a good example, and an attitude of togetherness do more to promote a harmonious learning environment than anything else we could ever do. If you can implement some of the simple family ideas discussed in the next several chapters, your success rate with the financial lessons in the rest of this book will increase dramatically.

Chapter Challenge ....

Sit down with your family for thirty minutes and discuss the statistics listed in chapter 2 about personal debt. Visit KPM.com and print out Form CC-3. Fill it out and insert it in your journal. Ask the question "What do you think will happen if these numbers continue to go up?" Write some of the responses in your journal. Talk about any examples you know that will illustrate the effects of personal debt in someone's life. Take the time to review any personal experiences you may have had with debt and the effect that situation may have had on your life. Record any interesting comments that come out of this discussion in your journal.

....

CHAPTER 4

How's Your Example?

*Live so that when your children think of fairness
and integrity, they think of you.*

—H. Jackson Brown, Jr.

THE *AMERICAN HERITAGE DICTIONARY* DEFINES "EXAMPLE" AS "someone or something worthy of imitation or duplication; a model; a pattern; exemplar." So, are we? How do we act in the privacy of our own homes? How do we speak to others in our family? What level of respect is shown to the other people who live in our house? Do we speak kindly about others when they aren't around to hear us? How much time and effort do we invest in enhancing our family relationships?

These questions are asked to illustrate a point. If you don't provide family members with the leadership and examples they need, you'll never have their attention or respect long enough to teach lesson one about financial literacy. Everything parents do in the home is observed and evaluated by those who look up to us. As the family leader, we parents set the pace for the rest of the family. If we're ambitious, so will be our children; if we're caring, so will be our children; if we're happy, so will be our children.

Because this book deals specifically with financial education in the home, we have to take an honest look at the financial example we are setting for our family members. There are five key components to our financial health:

1. Income

2. Expenses

3. Debt

4. Savings

5. Investment

Each of these components plays an important role in our effectiveness both as a family leader and as a member of society. While one component is not substantially more important than another, they do tend to work together to establish an overall financial momentum for your household. Let's take a look at each component separately.

Income

How much do you make? Do you work at more than one job? Are you happy with your career choice? Is there something else you would rather be doing? Has education limited your ability to get the kind of job you would like to have? Is there anything you could do *right now* to make a difference in your income level? The answers to these questions will reveal a great deal about you, your potential, and any action you may consider.

More income isn't always the solution. Many of us are probably very happy with our career choices. A number of us have been able to follow a rewarding career path, and we wouldn't dream of making a change. This state of gratitude usually is conducive to a satisfying family and financial experience.

If, however, we are unsatisfied, we will tend to manifest these feelings to those around us, both at work and at home. If we have the ability to create change, we need to determine what may be holding us back from making a change. If we have the ability to create more income for our family but choose not to leave our comfort zone to explore new opportunities, what is the impact on our family? We must deal with these issues if we are to be truly happy in our life's journey. It is up to us to make a difference, make a change, and make life good for those who depend on us. We must consider what decision we can make right now to effect a lasting change to enhance our financial environment and the example we are setting.

Expenses

No matter how much you earn, you'll always be able to outspend yourself. This is a lesson I learned years ago when my family transitioned from Air Force life to civilian life.

When I left the service in the late 1980s, I was fortunate enough to secure a position with a regional brokerage firm and start a career as a retail stockbroker. My business grew rapidly, and I enjoyed success almost immediately. Our family income increased dramatically over what I had made in the Air Force, and we were on top of the world. As the success continued, we started to live it up. We bought a bigger house, better cars, a boat, nicer clothes, private schools for the kids, the works!

It didn't take long to notice that even though we were making a lot more money, we were winding up with more month left at the end of the money. We were spending more than we were making and felt the stress of not having enough cash. We were setting a poor example for our kids. Since that time we've learned that no matter what our income, we have to budget below what we make. Whether we were in the Air Force making very little or in the brokerage business making a lot, none of it matters if our spending isn't controlled.

The best way to control spending is to set up a family budget and stick to it. This can be as simple as figuring out the monthly income, listing all expenses, subtracting one from the other, and then saving as much of what's left over as possible. By using a budgeting system, you will quickly gain control over your spending and will notice an increase in both cash available and peace of mind in your home. Financial instability is one of the leading causes of marital strife, and it will quickly destroy a family if not controlled.

Having a family budget is also a great way to build a teamlike environment in the home. A family budget is something that every member can participate in. By working on the budget as a family, each member will learn and grow through the experience. By using a family budgeting system, children will begin to understand the importance of financial management by example and parents will enjoy the peace associated with financial discipline. Figure 4-1 presents a basic budget sheet.

As you can see, we've covered a lot of ground in just a few lines. By detailing your income and expenses, you'll get a quick and clear picture of your immediate financial status. By making an effort and taking the time to fill out your budget every month, your cash flow will become very tangible.

Keeping a budget will help you avoid the trap of taking money for granted. The closer you monitor your monthly expenses now, the greater your reward will be in later years. Today, cash flow is supplied by the work that you do. Tomorrow, it will have to be supplied by the interest on the money you have invested. Make sure you have the investment to live on tomorrow by starting a budget today.

Usually you'll want to fill out your budget sheet during the first week of a new month. By doing so, you'll be able to update the previous month's "actual" numbers and make any "projected" budget number changes for the upcoming month. No matter when you choose to fill out your budget form, remember that you're doing better than over 90% of the world by simply having a budget and controlling your expenses.

FIGURE 4-1

BASIC BUDGET SHEET

Month _____   Year _____

INCOME

	PROJECTED	ACTUAL
Income #1	_____	_____
Income #2	_____	_____
Mail Money*	_____	_____
Other Income	_____	_____
Other Income	_____	_____
TOTAL INCOME (1)	_____	_____

EXPENSES

	PROJECTED	ACTUAL
Rent or Mortgage	_____	_____
2nd Mortgage	_____	_____
Condo Fee	_____	_____
Gas and Heat	_____	_____
Electric	_____	_____
Water	_____	_____
Telephone	_____	_____
Cable	_____	_____
Trash Removal	_____	_____
Groceries	_____	_____
Household Supplies	_____	_____
Dining Out	_____	_____

FIGURE 4-1   *(Continued)*

	PROJECTED	ACTUAL
Auto Payment 1	_____	_____
Auto Payment 2	_____	_____
Gas/Oil	_____	_____
Auto Maintenance	_____	_____
Parking	_____	_____
Public Transportation	_____	_____
Life Insurance	_____	_____
Health Insurance	_____	_____
Disability Insurance	_____	_____
Homeowners/Renters Insurance	_____	_____
Auto Insurance	_____	_____
Property Taxes	_____	_____
Income Taxes	_____	_____
Clothing Purchases	_____	_____
Laundry/Dry Cleaning	_____	_____
General Medical	_____	_____
Dental/Eye Care	_____	_____
Medications	_____	_____
Child Care/Tuition	_____	_____
Alimony/Child Support	_____	_____
Cosmetics/Hair Care	_____	_____
Tobacco/Alcohol	_____	_____
Books/Papers/Magazines	_____	_____
Gifts	_____	_____
Church/Dues/Charity	_____	_____
Other	_____	_____

FIGURE 4-1 *(Continued)*

	PROJECTED	ACTUAL
Entertainment		
Vacation Fund		
Credit Card 1		
Credit Card 2		
Credit Card 3		
Loan 1		
Loan 2		
Loan 3		
TOTAL EXPENSES (2)		

EMPOWER

	PROJECTED	ACTUAL
TOTAL INCOME (1)		
LESS TOTAL EXPENSES (2)		
WHAT'S LEFT OVER		

What are you going to do with it?

1. To Debt Elimination: $_____
2. To Emergency Fund: $_____
3. To Retirement Fund: $_____
4. To Savings: $_____

*Mail Money is income derived from activities and investments outside of your primary source of income. This could include rental property income, stock dividends, interest on loans made, and multilevel marketing activities.

Debt

Part of any effective budgeting system should be the systematic elimination of debt. Credit card debt is the most hazardous because of how easy it is to accumulate and because of its high interest rate. If you carry any credit card debt, eliminate it as quickly as possible. Try to pay more than the minimum payment each month and accelerate your payoff. Once you've paid off the credit card, use the card sparingly and make sure you don't charge more than you can pay off at one time. Credit cards are important for travel and emergencies, so most people need to have access to them, but be disciplined in how you use them.

Once your credit card debt is gone, chip away at any other debt you may have. It's good to own your car outright, and there is no greater feeling than owning your home free and clear. The best example for your children is to see that of a debt-free parent making the most of life.

If you happen to have a variety of debts outstanding that you would like to eliminate, Figure 4-2 will be helpful. A friend of mine, Dave Ramsey, calls this the "Debt Snowball," and it works like this.

To start, you'll want to list all debts that you want to eliminate from the smallest to largest. Each of these debts will have a minimum monthly payment that needs to be maintained through your budget.

Once your budget is up and running, you should show an excess (hopefully) of funds at the end of the month. Take that excess and attack your smallest debt with a vengeance. As soon as that debt is gone, get to work on the next one in line, and so on. Each time you eliminate a debt, you'll also eliminate its monthly payment, which will increase your bottom line on your budget, which will give you more money to pulverize more debts.

Once all your debt is gone (How do you think you'll feel then?), keep it gone. Take those dollars and get them working for you.

Figure 4-2

DEBT ELIMINATION SCHEDULE

Date Started _____

List all debts from smallest to largest.

Creditor	Balance	Will be Gone by:	Did It!
1. _____	$_____	___/___/___	___/___/___
2. _____	$_____	___/___/___	___/___/___
3. _____	$_____	___/___/___	___/___/___
4. _____	$_____	___/___/___	___/___/___
5. _____	$_____	___/___/___	___/___/___
6. _____	$_____	___/___/___	___/___/___
7. _____	$_____	___/___/___	___/___/___
8. _____	$_____	___/___/___	___/___/___
9. _____	$_____	___/___/___	___/___/___
TOTAL DEBT	$_____	___/___/___	___/___/___

Now you're *free. You* call the shots!

There are no traffic jams along the extra mile.

—Roger Staubach

Always remember what an old farmer once said about interest, "Thems that knows it, makes it; thems that don't, pays it."

Savings

Over the course of a lifetime, people have a number of different savings objectives. One of the most basic is the family emergency fund. Initially, this fund should be enough to sustain your family for one month without income. As you increase your savings prowess, you will want to increase the account to cover from six months' to a year's worth of expenses. The family emergency account will add a buffer that will enhance the safety and security felt by every family member.

Once you've established the emergency fund, you should begin to maximize your retirement savings. If you have a 401(k) through your employer, maximize your contributions. If not, maximize your deposits to an IRA or other qualified tax-deferred retirement vehicle. You should plan to maximize your qualified retirement investment before you make any outside investment decision. Consider speaking with an accountant or tax attorney before you make any tax-related investment.

Investment

Once you have eliminated your personal debt, established an emergency fund, and maximized your retirement contributions, you're ready to start investing any excess income.

I probably should clarify the difference between savings and investment. Savings are dollars that you should be able to access on relatively short notice (three to six months). Investment is indicative of a long-term commitment. An investor should carefully consider each investment and should make investment decisions based on an intention to hold the security for an extended period of time (years as opposed to days). In fact, you should take as long researching an investment as it took you to earn the dollars being invested.

I discuss investment philosophy in greater detail in later chapters. For now, it's important for you to understand the effect your investment decisions will have on your children. If you are in a financial position to make investments, your children are lucky to have you as an example. Share with them your experiences, and let them see what it is like to have control over your financial accounts. You are their greatest source of knowledge and encouragement; give them all you can.

Make sure that the five key components to your financial example are working in harmony. Also, be sure you're working in the right field of endeavor to maximize your personal potential. If you are unhappy or dissatisfied with your current employment situation, only you can make the decision to change it. Budget your expenses, establish your family emergency fund, and establish a saving and investment plan for your discretionary income. As you begin to put your financial house in order, you'll discover a peace and harmony in your home that you've never known. Even initially, as you plan out your financial objectives, you'll notice a personal strength growing within you. Your countenance will change, your confidence will increase, and your family will notice.

Chapter Challenge ....

Sit down with your spouse and review each of the five components to your financial example together. Discuss how each could be improved and how each affects the example you are setting for your children. Visit KPM.com, print out Form CC-4, and complete it. Hole-punch the form and insert it into your journal. Set some personal financial goals and resolve to make a lasting change. Write down at least one task that you can do immediately to make a difference. Record this commitment in your journal.

....

CHAPTER 5

How's Your Communication?

If you want your children to turn out well, spend twice as much time with them and half as much money.

—Anonymous

In the last chapter, we discussed ways in which you can be an example to your children. Once you have established yourself as a strong financial example, you'll want to take a detailed look at your family communication skills. One of the most important elements to establishing a strong family unit is the ability to talk openly and freely with each other. The level at which your family communicates will have a significant impact on your ability to problem-solve effectively and teach financial intelligence within the home.

One of the greatest skills you can develop in your family is the ability to listen. It seems as if today too many people spend too much time trying to be heard by everybody around them. People have a tendency to express themselves and make sure that they say whatever it is that they need to get out, whether anyone is listening or not. How many times have you been in a discussion with a family member where the other person is speaking to you but your brain is busy contemplating your reply? In most families this happens often and is recognized as the basic ingredient to ineffective communication.

As Stephen Covey, author of the national bestseller *The 7 Habits of Highly Effective People,* so eloquently put it, "Seek first to understand, then to be understood." Should we choose to listen first and speak second, we would all enjoy more effective and satisfying conversations with one another. Not only that, but what we say actually may sink in and get considered by those we're talking to.

Here are a few suggestions to help you enhance the communication process within your family:

1. Try to use words and actions that make the person who is talking feel as if he or she is important and is being heard.

2. If a child or spouse approaches you to say something, stop what you are doing and look directly at him or her while they are speaking.

3. After the person is done speaking, repeat back what you think he or she is trying to say, and then respond accordingly.

4. Try to avoid criticism or harsh words and maintain a loving and nurturing demeanor. Speak softly and slowly to maintain a peaceful disposition and keep yourself calm.

5. Use positive body language. Hugs and hand-holding are especially important for spouses and children through the developmental ages.

6. Be respectful at all times while communicating. If something disagreeable is said, take a couple of deep breaths before responding. Once calm, respond in a lower, slower tone.

Effective communication skills are at the heart of a successful family experience. All family members need to feel comfortable in stating how they feel without fear of judgment or criticism. There will never be a better opportunity than right now to sit down with your family and discuss how to discuss. Good luck!

Chapter Challenge ....

Visit KPM.com and print out Form CC-5, fill it out, and insert it into your journal. Sit down with your family and discuss your family communication skills. Review the six effective communication techniques mentioned in this chapter and discuss them with your family. Write the results and details of your conversation in your journal. The next time you become involved in a family disagreement, become aware of your countenance and practice emotional control. When you respond to the person you are talking to, imagine them as your favorite grandparent or a good friend. How would this response tactic enhance your communication effectiveness and maintain a degree of harmony in your home? Write any thoughts you may have in your journal.

....

CHAPTER 6

Developing a Family Mission Statement

The future belongs to those who see the possibilities before they become obvious.

—Anonymous

Most successful organizations with an effective business plan also have a mission statement. This statement defines a company's objectives and serves as a standard by which corporate decisions can be made and evaluated. An effective mission statement clearly defines the organization's destination and effectively serves as a rudder to keep the entity on track.

Most companies were founded with a purpose in mind and have charted a preliminary course toward that objective. The degree to which they can stay on track is a measure of its effectiveness. As long as the organization is fairly close to the charted line, it is operating effectively and carries a degree of momentum toward its destination. The farther the firm deviates from its charted course, the less effective it is, and accumulated momentum diminishes. Three steps create the ultimate course of action:

1. A clearly defined starting point

2. A clearly defined destination

3. A tangible plan to get from one point to the other

The family mission statement is what can keep a family on course. If everyone is clear on the direction in which the family is moving, there will be little question as to which course of action to choose. Once this commitment is in place, it can eliminate doubt, create stability, and give every member of the family team a sense of belonging, meaning, and direction.

A family mission statement can be something as simple as "to get along together, be happy, and minimize conflict." Any issues that come up can be resolved by considering them in light of the mission statement. Does this action take us closer to, or farther from, our desired outcome?

You may choose to create a more elaborate statement than this one. Yours may define family objectives and integrate each member's detailed participation. Whether complex or simple, this personal constitution will become an important element in creating a bond that will keep the family motivated, together, and moving forward.

When putting your family mission statement together, the first step is to sit down and discuss some of the following questions.

- What is important to you as a member of this family?

- What can you do to help the family as a whole?

- What do you think your greatest strengths are?

- What are some weaknesses you may need to work on?

- What can other family members do to help you?

- What do you think our family goal should be?

If you visit KPM.com, you'll see that Form FMS-1 will give you a template that includes these questions to help you construct your family mission statement.

Be open and honest and allow each member to speak freely. You may want to challenge your family to contemplate these questions for a day or two and then meet again to review the answers. By asking these questions and positioning each family member as an important member of the statement writing team, you will foster a degree of togetherness by designing a common family goal. Each family member will feel that they were an important part in the development of a document that provides a clear definition of what your family is all about.

Once you've had a chance to review everyone's responses, you'll begin to see how each member can best contribute to overall family objectives. You may want to include specific words or phrases from each member's answer when formulating the statement. Again, this will foster a feeling of significance and unification in the family experience.

Once you've reviewed everyone's responses and picked out individual words or phrases, you'll want to write a rough draft of the statement. Don't worry about how it looks initially; just write down several sentences that include family members' responses in your journal. Once you've done this, sit down as a family to review the rough draft with everyone. Members will give you input and offer suggestions that will help you edit and clarify the final draft. If you use the journal for this process, you'll have a record of how your constitution came together.

Once you finish the family mission statement, make sure every family member gets a copy. This simple document should be a helpful, unifying, and meaningful motivator to your family's overall success and achievement.

Chapter Challenge ....

Bring your family together and discuss the family mission questions listed in this chapter. Design your family mission statement, and ask for individual ideas from your family members. Write a rough draft of the document in your journal, review it with your family, and make any necessary revisions. Neatly write out a final version and make sure everyone in the family gets a copy. As your family grows and changes, you may want to update this document. The journal can help you remember your family focus and will serve as a reminder to you as things change.

. . . .

CHAPTER 7

....

Do You Feel Like a Team or What?

There is no self-made man; you will reach your goals only with the help of others.

—George Shinn

I HOPE THAT, AFTER THE LAST THREE CHAPTERS, YOU'RE BEGINNING to feel like the captain of a sports team. You have started to communicate more effectively, you're setting a better example, and you've got a family mission statement to go by. All of these important factors will work together for the family's benefit and for you personally, as the family leader.

The sense of belonging to something meaningful is an essential element in the success and unity of every family. If you observe what goes on in the street gangs across the country, you will find that it's the sense of belonging that lures the children into the gang in the first place. This sense of belonging is a powerful force as children mature; you want to make sure it is working *for* your family, not *against* it.

One of the most meaningful family bonds you can create for your children is to make them feel as if they belong to something special. The family mission statement will help with this to a certain degree, but it's only part of the plan. The purpose of this book is to help you teach your children basic financial intelligence in a comfortable and nurturing family environment. As you and your family progress through the financial intelligence concepts, you'll see that your children's actions will play a vital role in the overall effectiveness of your family experience. By helping your children realize that they are important contributors to the family mission, they will discover an overwhelming sense of belonging. Once they find this belonging within their own home, they won't bother to look elsewhere to satisfy the need.

Besides the family mission statement, one of the things you can do to enhance your children's sense of belonging is to develop a family motto. This simple phrase is different from the mission statement; it is a very brief statement that has a special meaning to each family team member. Where a family mission statement may be several paragraphs, a family motto is only a few words.

This motto will help your family create its own unique identity among other families in your community. My grandmother was a descendant of the Kennedy family from Scotland. Their motto, *Avis la Fin,* roughly translates to "Consider the End." This important consideration has helped many a Kennedy family member through difficult personal decisions. *Avis la Fin* was a family theme that helped the Kennedys differentiate themselves from other Scottish families and promoted a high degree of unity among Kennedy family members. Along with their motto, the Kennedy family had a unique family crest and plaid pattern specific to their name. The Kennedys were proud of their name and heritage; the family motto, crest, and plaid helped foster this pride.

Developing your own family motto can be a fun and rewarding endeavor. Begin by sitting down with your family to talk about your family feeling. How does it feel to be part of your family? What are the common traits to your family membership? Brainstorm key words and phrases that have special meaning to the members of your family team.

One helpful suggestion may be to do a little genealogy research to see if there is already a family motto somewhere in your family history. If you choose to investigate your family, the history you discover will become a substantial part of defining what your family stands for. When you research and discover your family history and then link that history to your current family, you create family pride, a lasting bond, and sense of belonging that is difficult to break.

With the prevalence of blended, step, adoptive, and foster families, genealogy takes on new significance. Everyone needs to understand their personal roots. We all have a genetic mother and father. We all also have a parental figure that played an important role in raising us. Many questions about who we are can be answered by tracking down where we came from.

It's important for us as individuals to have a clear distinction of our roots and history. While some of it may be painful and a bit confusing, it's important for each of us to have a clear understanding of our origin. The truth about who we are and where we came from will only serve us throughout our lifetimes. As we are honest with the ones we care for, we establish a foundation upon which we can build. Help your children understand their roots and the important role they play in your family, regardless of their genetic origins.

By spending the time to research your family history, you will give your children a defining piece of information about themselves. This information gives them a special assurance and a peace of mind that will permeate their everyday life experience. This historical family information will give your children the roots they may have been missing. The deeper and more broadly based your children's roots are, the less likely they will be to sway or be knocked over by the storms and winds of life.

You can help your children discover their roots and family motto, or you can design one of your own. Help your children to understand that the family name is something to be proud of and that they are a part of something very unique and special.

Chapter Challenge ....

Visit KPM.com and print out Form CC-7. This will help construct the first two generations of your family tree. Investigate your family roots and put together a family tree going back to at least your grandparents. Do a bit of research and see if your family name has a history to it. Go to the Internet site www.familysearch.org and enter your parents' information. It's likely that you'll find out about their parents, their grandparents, and so on. It will be an exciting on-line adventure for your whole family. Ask your oldest generation if you have a family motto in your history. If you don't discover one, design one that is meaningful and that will serve to remind all family members how important your family name is. Record any information you discover in your journal. You may even choose to illustrate your family tree as you write.

....

CHAPTER 8

Family Financial Habits

*What we do today, right now, will have an accumulated
effect on all our tomorrows.*

—ALEXANDRIA STODDARD

WHAT ARE YOUR FAMILY'S FINANCIAL HABITS? HOW DO YOU MAKE
financial decisions? What are your spending habits? Do you use a
budget? Do you finance your toys? Are you saving? Do you have
an emergency fund? How's your impulse buying? Have you ever
heard of "gratification deferral"? The answers to these questions
will tell a great deal about your family's level of financial intelligence and spending discipline. Each of your answers will help you
assess your current philosophy and give you insight into issues
you may want to modify. In order to create a more structured and
viable financial plan, you will need to examine your current
financial habits.

Each of us, over the years, has developed a number of positive
and negative financial habits. This evolution has been a result of a
combination of circumstances, nurturing, education, and experiences. Many times our financial habits are based on what money
we've been able to earn, on what we can buy as a result of those
earnings, and, for some, on the borrowing potential those earnings

create. Many people don't even think about their financial habits; they simply live from hand to mouth, month after month.

The financial habits that we propagate will be the primary determinant of the success and security we will enjoy in our later years. If we implement a degree of discipline, maximize our earnings potential by doing our best, watch our spending, and save for the future, we are likely to enjoy a fruitful life. If we are careless and allow our emotions to rule our financial decisions, we may very well be in for a long and stressful life journey. The key to creating strong financial habits is to recognize the need for a personal financial plan and then to develop the discipline needed to design and implement that plan.

There are four main elements to consider in every personal financial plan:

1. Your goal

2. Your income

3. Your expenses

4. Your savings

Let's look at each one separately.

Your Goal

As simple as it is, a goal is something most families do not have. Most families today are so caught up in their daily activities, they don't even know where they are going. By having a goal, you have a destination. This destination is what you expect out of life. A goal must be specific; it must be adequate for your needs; and it must be attainable by a predetermined date. For example, if you want to make sure each of your kids gets to college and still retire when you're age fifty-five with an income of at least $50,000 per year, state that. Once you know where you want to be, you can then calculate what you have to do to get there. In your goal attainment calculations, make sure to include every source of income and every expense along the way. There's nothing like working all your life toward a specific monetary goal only to find out that you're 10% under where you really need to be.

The following goal attainment formula may be helpful; it can be reproduced from KPM.com as Form GAF-1:

My personal goal is _____, and I hope to have it accomplished by _____. In order for me to reach this objective, I'll need to save approximately $_____ by the accomplishment date. This means that I'll have to save at least $_____ per _____ to reach the objective.

In the case of a nonmonetary objective, you may want to try the following:

My personal goal is _____, and I hope to accomplish it by _____. In order to reach this objective, I'll have to complete the following steps.

1. _____
2. _____
3. _____
4. _____
5. _____

My most formidable challenge in attaining this goal is _____, so I'll have to be particularly diligent when accomplishing this step. I know I can make it, and as the motivational speaker Brian Tracy once said, "If it's going to be, it's up to me."

Your Income

What is your current income, and what will you be able to earn if you switch to another job? Are you being compensated adequately for your skills, or will other opportunities allow you more flexibility and benefits? What can you do to increase your value to your employer? What can you do to increase your value to your industry? Do you have an opportunity to strike out and establish your own company?

No matter what your employment situation is now, you must remember that you always have complete control over your income and the number of opportunities that present themselves to you. The only difference between you and the independently wealthy Internet entrepreneur is the decisions you each have made. If you condition your mind for success, there's nothing that you won't be able to accomplish. The greatest assets you have are your mind and your imagination. Remember what Albert Einstein said: "Imagination is more powerful than knowledge." Use your imagination to create more income.

Your Expenses

How much do you spend every week on unnecessary purchases? How much do you spend eating away from home? How often do you pick up impulse items on your way to a necessary purchase? Do you own a new car but are still renting an apartment? Is your house payment reasonable compared to your personal income? By answering these questions honestly, you will see your spending style.

When it comes to affluence, looks can be deceiving. People who drive nice cars, live in beautiful homes, and belong to the right clubs may have very little disposable income. They live from month to month, trying desperately to survive and keep up with the expenses they have incurred. Others who live in modest homes, drive used cars, and go bowling with their kids wind up being the millionaires next door.

Your Savings

So, you've set your financial goals; you're maximizing your contribution to society through industrious effort; you spend only on the necessities because your self-esteem enables you not to have to keep up with the neighbors. Now you need to figure out what to do with all the extra cash. Congratulations! You're on your way to financial freedom through a sound and lasting set of family financial habits.

There are a number of different savings and investment accounts that you'll need to be familiar with. We'll go into detail about each, but for your convenience, below is a list of the various savings and investment accounts that you'll consider throughout your lifetime:

1. The emergency fund, 1–6 months of income just in case.

2. Your retirement, the first place to save because it's tax-deferred.

3. College savings for your children, let them help out on this one.

4. Your investment account, saving is not investing, go direct.

Each account has a different purpose, and each will be an important part of your overall financial plan. By simply establishing your emergency fund, you'll be doing better than most of your neighbors. It's a small commitment, but it will give you peace of mind worth ten times the account value. This account should be enough to cover your monthly budget for one to six months, depending on your savings abilities. Once this fund is established, you'll have a level of safety that will enable you to consider alternative, less liquid investments.

Your first savings commitment after your emergency fund should be with a tax-deferred retirement plan like an individual retirement account (IRA) or 401(k). If you're saving money through certificates of deposit, a money market account, or simple passbook savings, Uncle Sam's gonna tax your interest income. The same goes for fixed income securities such as bonds or mutual funds with a high dividend. If you like the excitement of trading, especially online, you'll wind up paying a capital gains tax on your increase. The only way to avoid these tax consequences is to do your saving, investing, and trading in a qualified account like an IRA or Keogh plan.

The long-term results of compounded, tax-deferred savings are significant. Consider an initial investment of $10,000 with an annual return of 11% (the average return of the market since 1926) over a period of thirty years. If you used a conventional growth mutual fund and were taxed on the capital gains and interest, after thirty years your balance would be $98,414. If, on the other hand, you had the same investment in a qualified plan, your balance after thirty years would be $228,922.

Simply by investing in a qualified plan first, you'll have an extra $130,508 earning income for you when you need it. Put another way, your retirement income will be $870 a month higher if you make some very simple and intelligent decisions today.

Once you've maximized your annual contribution to those retirement vehicles, if you still have money left over (congratulations), you'll want to check out some investment opportunities with a local broker. You're probably not going to be a huge player in the market right away, so it's prudent to choose a good-quality, no-load growth mutual fund. With a mutual fund you can invest small amounts of money and still benefit from diversification and professional management.

A number of great resources are available to help you make decisions regarding what fund to choose. One of the biggest mistakes investors make is selecting last year's high-performing fund as this year's big winner. Every fund manager will have a great year and every great fund manager will have a doggy year. Because of the effects of market fluctuation and managers' needs for self-preservation, one kind of year usually follows the other.

In selecting a fund, make sure you look at the five- and ten-year performance numbers as well as the manager's tenure. You also may wish to review the fund's rating by Morningstar at www.morningstar.net or Value Line at www.valueline.com. These publications also can be found through your local library if you don't have access to the Internet. Either resource will give you detailed and objective information about most mutual funds available to date. If a fund's review is positive, the numbers are good, and the manager has been around for a while, you've probably found a good long-term investment.

If you can get to a point where you have set some specific financial objectives and have at least established an emergency fund, you're ahead of 95% of the rest of the population. The steps outlined in this chapter are very broad and should provide you with some basic ideas. Implementing every aspect of a savings and investment plan could take some time. Give yourself some slack and don't expect to accomplish everything overnight. Life is a marathon, not a sprint. Start out slow, plan your pace, stick to it, and be there for the finish line.

Chapter Challenge ....

Set aside an hour to discuss your family's financial goals. Review your income and spending habits and establish plans for a family emergency fund. Then take a minute to review your retirement funds (IRA, Keogh, or 401(k)) and make sure you're maximizing your contributions and investment selections. Make sure your family's financial objectives are specific and write them down. Decide what you need to do first and jot down the first step in your personal financial plan process. (This probably will be your emergency fund.) Determine an initial family financial objective and commit to attaining that goal. Go to KPM.com and print out Form CC-8. This form will help you clarify your financial situation and should help you get started on a progressive path to financial security.

....

CHAPTER 9

Helping Your Children Reach Their Greatest Potential

Keep away from people who try to belittle your ambitions.
Small people always do that, but the really great
make you feel that you, too, are great.

—MARK TWAIN

EACH TOPIC WE'VE REVIEWED SO FAR HAS BEEN PREPARATORY TO the process of teaching your children effective financial principles. By now you've developed a personal financial plan; you have an idea of what it takes to be a good example to your children; and you have a better understanding of how to communicate more effectively with your children. You've designed a family mission statement and have created a team spirit atmosphere in the home through your family motto. You've accomplished the necessary groundwork to prepare a family environment that is conducive to family and financial lessons. This environment is absolutely necessary if your children are ever to have the financial intelligence they will need to navigate real-world issues.

As you and I both know, the real world can be a tough place to make mistakes. Trial and error is no way to go through life when there are real dollars and lives at stake. As parents, we have the opportunity to give our children a degree of real-life experience while they are still living in the comfort and safety of our homes. Real-life experience can be gained most safely in a place where mistakes are acceptable and where caring parents can help correct any problems. Our kids should have an understanding of financial responsibility and of how the real world works before they get there. This learning process will not take place anywhere else but in the home; the only way our children will gain financial experience is if we, the parents, help them. We need to let our children experience the life lessons of opportunity, responsibility, consequence, effort, reward, and achievement. The following seven steps are designed specifically for that purpose and will help your children attain financial intelligence.

These seven steps were developed over a number of years through my experience at Cash University. Their mention here represents an outline of the remainder of this book and should serve to help you better understand how the components work together for your family's benefit. By following these seven steps, you'll have the tools necessary to foster a happier and more organized educational environment in your home.

Step 1: Know the Rules

The first thing we must do as leaders of a family team is to make sure our players know all the rules. This sounds simple enough, but few parents actually take the time to discuss the household rules and responsibilities with their children. Most parents just assume that the kids will figure it out for themselves. But, if a child doesn't know what is expected as a family member or what the household rules are, he or she is walking in a minefield. For both kids and adults, defined expectations create boundaries, which means safety. If we didn't have traffic rules and regulations, how many of us would venture out for groceries during the day? The same concept holds true for our children at home. They need to know that there is order in life and where they specifically fit in.

Step 2: Set Your Objectives

Just as parents need their own financial objectives, kids need goals too. Goals are an excellent way to create focus and excitement for the child. Goals provide the motivation behind why other jobs get done. Goals answer the whys of life. If you enable your children to attain their goals through effort, you've just added dynamically to their self-image and self-esteem. Goals become the driving force in life and accomplishment becomes the reward.

Step 3: Look for Opportunity

I mentioned that it is important to enable children to attain their goals. It also is important to create an environment that prepares them for the real world. How can we help our children to reach their goals through a real-life goal attainment process? We can provide them with an opportunity to earn their objective through good old-fashioned effort and reward. This principle has grown to become less popular among today's youth, but it's really the only way I've ever seen adults acquire any sort of income. Because of this, we need to teach our kids how to earn, how to look for opportunity, and how to be excited about their limitless potential. This is exciting, and our kids need to experience it firsthand.

By giving our children a chance to earn and save, we enable them to develop self-esteem and a pride of ownership when they obtain their goal. As parents, we're the only ones that can give our children this achievement opportunity. They need to comprehend that the world represents a great opportunity to grow and develop and is not a place to fear.

Step 4: Be Aware of Your Emotions

As parents we are supposed to be fair, reasonable, unbiased, non-judgmental, and responsible examples to our children. Responsible means we are able to choose our response. However, often we don't. Instead, we spout off whatever our emotions dictate in a time of crisis. "How many times have I told you not to . . .?" "Why the heck did you ever . . . ?" "What in the world is wrong with you?" "Why is he crying?" "Put this *@&% away *now*!" Does any of this sound familiar? Rather than responding in anger, it is far better for us, as parents, to take a few deep breaths, maybe a little time, and then address the issue. Otherwise, we wind up looking a bit stupid in front of our children, spouses, friends, and, sometimes, neighbors.

The topic of emotional control becomes much simpler when we have established the rules of the game beforehand. By letting our team players know what is expected up front, we minimize the emotional element on the other end. If we have established the rule "Do not smack your brother" and have assigned a consequence of a 50-cent deduction in any weekly earnings, the next time brother gets smacked we unemotionally deduct the 50 cents from any money earned that week. Now, of course, we want to help the offending child avoid such behavior in the future, and we may choose to have a nice long talk about what happened. But the key is that emotions are kept out of situations and parent and child can openly discuss what happened and how to avoid such a consequence in the future.

Step 5: Saving and Personal Record Keeping

Saving and record keeping is a fun subject because it represents the nuts and bolts of how the seven steps can work in your home. In chapter 29 you'll learn how to design several charts that will help you to keep track of your children's weekly earnings. On the same chart, you'll track the household rules and any of their consequences. I'll also talk about goal setting and how to create a visual reminder of your children's goal items. You'll want to keep your children motivated toward goal attainment. In chapter 35 you'll see how to put together a children's checkbook that can be used to track where their money came from and where it went. I'll also talk about enhancing your family journal as well as personal journals. Journal writing represents a wonderful opportunity to reflect on the day's events, how they affected you, and what they mean to your family.

Step 6: Goal Attainment, the Cornerstone of Self-Esteem

In this step we discuss what happens when we attain our goals, the terrific feelings of accomplishment, and the pride that accompanies such events.

Goal attainment gives parents the opportunity to praise their children like never before. We can really make a difference in the lives of our kids by letting them know just how proud we are of their accomplishments.

Our children will benefit in the pride of ownership that accompanies buying something with their own hard-earned dollars. It has been my experience that attained goal items are not left around to be ruined; they're not lent to friends; and they are taken care of better than other possessions that children may have.

Goal attainment also allows children and the parents to discuss the process by which the goal was attained—whether it was easy and what could have been done differently in the process. Goal attainment also allows the parents and children the opportunity to discuss new and more substantial goal items to begin working toward.

In chapter 44 I'll also discuss the importance of helping others. Giving back, not just monetarily, is an important principle for children to understand as they grow. The happiness that accompanies going out of your way to help someone else cannot be measured in financial terms.

Step 7: Attain Again

In step 7 we review the events that took place throughout the program. It's important for parents to understand clearly what is taking place in their homes and to notice any behavioral changes that are occurring.

As your family goes through the seven-step process, many good things will happen. Children will be more open to communication and will be more conscious of the events that are going on around them. You'll notice that the "gimmes" will go away and overall behavior will improve. As they become more responsible, they will develop a more positive self-image and will desire to participate more in household activities. The level and depth of family communication will improve dramatically, and you will find yourselves discussing topics and events that you never could have imagined.

As the family team leader, you have the opportunity to make a great difference in the lives of your family members. The detail within the seven steps will provide guidelines to help you and your family members reach their greatest potential. As you grow and learn together, you will find a happiness that you have never known. As you spend more time with your family, relationships will be enhanced, special activities will be more frequent and more enjoyable, and a feeling of peace will pervade the home.

Chapter Challenge ....

Gather all of your family team members together and, taking turns, read this chapter aloud. After you're done, discuss the contents and answer any questions family members may have. Explain that you'll be working with them from now on to help them accomplish their objectives and that you want this to be a fun and exciting experience for everyone involved.

....

KNOW THE RULES

CHAPTER 10

....

What Rules
Are For

*Leaders are made, they are not born. They are made
by hard effort, which is the price we all must pay
to achieve any goal that is worthwhile.*

—VINCE LOMBARDI

EVERYTHING IN THIS WORLD IS GOVERNED BY LAWS. NATURE
has laws that cannot be violated. Science has laws that cannot be
violated. Society has laws that cannot be violated. Why should
your home be any different? In fact, I'll bet that it's not.

We all have rules to follow: me, you, my kids, and your kids.
One thing that I've found, however, is that kids are mostly igno-
rant and need to be taught everything! That's right. Children come
into this world with no prior knowledge, no programming, no
rule book to read before they walk and talk. Everything—good or
bad—that they know comes from us. Consequently, it's up to us
to determine how these new people turn out.

One of the most important things that we can do for our children is to teach them about family rules. Contrary to what most
teenagers will tell you, rules make people feel good, safe, secure,

and protected. If it weren't for rules, the car we drive would probably fall apart, the roads we drive on would be hazardous, and the food we eat could be toxic. Rules are good; they promote order and keep our world from falling apart.

Because we adults are smart and have gained life experience, we know why rules are important. The little people who live in our homes need this wisdom and will get it from only one place—us. How do we impart this wisdom to our little troublemakers? How, without violence and damaged self-esteem, do we help our kids understand what's appropriate and what's expected? The answer to these questions can be found in the next pages of this book.

Over the next several chapters, I will explain how to set appropriate boundaries for kids and how to explain the importance of family rules to the little people in our lives. We'll work on age-appropriate expectations, consistency, record keeping, and family responsibilities. The key to avoiding conflict in the home is to define what's okay and what's not and then discuss the consequences. If everybody understands the rules and consequences, nobody can get upset when a rule is violated or when a consequence is imposed.

Chapter Challenge ....

Talk about traffic rules with your kids and explain why they're important. Ask your children what would happen if we didn't have traffic rules and what it would be like to try to drive somewhere without any of these rules.

....

CHAPTER 11

Age-Appropriate Expectations and Development

Don't wrestle with pigs; you both get dirty and the pigs like it.

—MARK TWAIN

WHAT WAS THE FIRST WORD YOUR CHILD LEARNED? IF IT WASN'T *mama* or *dada*, I'll bet it was *no!* Babies are naturally inquisitive and will explore everything. They have no experience in anything and wind up testing parents daily. Baby rules (up to age one) are pretty simple: Watch every move they make and protect them from everything. It seems like we're always pulling them away from the top of the stairs or the base of the stove. If it's hot, sharp, unstable, or will stain, that's where your little person will decide to hang out. There's no need to go into baby expectations because there really aren't any. Simply keep them away from the dangerous stuff and give them all the love and affection you can muster.

At this point, to provide some background, I probably should discuss the importance of child development and self-concept. Self-concept begins very early in life and stems from the degree to which we think we are pleasing to our parents. Children live on praise and will do almost everything to get it. When praise is with-held, it's nearly impossible for children to feel good about themselves. Young children will begin to see themselves as failures when too many expectations are placed on them.

The toddler development stage lasts from ages one to three and is likely the most challenging stage of child development for parents. A tremendous amount of growth takes place, both physiologically and psychologically, during this time. Children will go from speaking only a few words at one year to speaking many words and phrases by thirty-six months. They will continue to be needy and dependent, but at the same time they will grow and develop into physically and emotionally independent people.

During this period parents notice children becoming more aware of themselves, more independent, and more assertive in interactions with parents and other children. "No," "I want," and "I need" are common phrases heard from toddlers. Children at this stage also test their assertiveness by telling parents what to do, how to do it, and when to do it. As parents, we need to be patient.

Eventually this assertiveness turns to anger and frustration when children are unable to accomplish what they're trying to do. When a parent sets a limit on a child's behavior, the child will likely react by yelling, hitting, and throwing things, including your basic temper tantrum. This physical assertiveness is children's way of releasing the tension that they cannot express in words. This physical assertiveness is normal, appropriate, and controllable in toddlers.

You can manage these outbreaks very easily by simply ignoring undesirable behavior, assigning a "time-out," or removing a privilege when an undesirable behavior occurs. These negative reinforcers will help children negotiate this stage of development and become more capable of achieving their emotional goals. By being consistent in your response to them, the tantrums and undesirable behavior eventually will decrease.

By the time children turn four, you should have a pretty good understanding of one another and your communication process should be fairly well established. At this point, children will start to become aware of "things" around them. They will also become aware that these things would be nice to have. The first manifestations of these feelings will appear in the grocery store, most likely in the checkout line when a church friend is behind you. As you shop for your family's necessities, your children may well have picked out some necessities of their own. "I want," "I need," "can I," and "Pleeeeese?" will be routine phrases heard in the store, particularly in the checkout line. (Kids really know when to push for the close.) I refer to this stage of development as the "gimme years."

The "gimme years," while mostly inconvenient, do provide an excellent opportunity for parents to begin discussing where things come from and how to get things for yourself. It may be easier to say "no" or "would you please put that down," but this wants-deficiency scenario represents an excellent opportunity to teach and learn.

The gimme years can last from age four to as long as the mid-thirties or later, depending on parental leniency. The longer the parent waits to teach basic financial principles and help children develop some degree of personal financial accountability, the more difficult it will be for children to break free and achieve financial independence.

From about age four, children start to comprehend material value. Once they begin to realize that "stuff is fun," they also must be shown the offsetting financial principles that govern the material world. It is during this critical time that children should be exposed to the basic financial principles of goal setting, opportunity, effort, and reward. If you explain these principles early on, thoughts of "something for nothing" won't have the chance to enter into the child's psychology.

By teaching children the skills necessary to set and attain goals on their own, you will help them to formulate their own financial independence objectives later in life. If you don't teach them about independence and destiny control at an early age, you may find that you've enabled them to hang on to the family purse. The longer children or young adults are allowed to be financed by parental support, the more difficult it will be for them to break away to independence. A study was recently conducted to determine what happens to young adults when they moved out of the home for the first time. The study results determined that the average number of days between move-out and move-back-in is only ninety days. The phrase "boomerang generation" accurately describes this unique phenomenon.

As children grow, they have the opportunity to learn many things in the home. They learn how to walk, talk, use the bathroom, be nice, and interact with others, especially the parent. One of the most important lessons that they will learn is the ability to understand and effectively negotiate the financial environment. As we've said, shopping represents a great financial needs classroom, and lots of really good experience can be gained there. A grocery store visit will be the basis of your children's financial reference frame. The earlier you can acclimate them to goal setting and earning, the more effective and less stressful the acclimation will be.

Enjoy your children's early development. Understand what they're going through, and help them to negotiate the early years with patience and understanding. When they begin to understand that "stuff is cool," help them to put "stuff acquisition" in its proper perspective. Give them the opportunity to set a goal for something they would like to have, and then help them save toward it. Show your children what it takes to make a purchase at the store, and then go through a checkbook-balancing lesson to show them where the money came from. Help your children understand these basic financial principles early on in the home so they don't have to experience them through trial and error by themselves later on.

Chapter Challenge ....

The next time you go to the store with your children, between the ages of four and ten, let them participate in the experience. Let them see the final bill and explain what it took to earn the dollars to pay the bill. Have them do a job around the house for ten or fifteen minutes. Explain that the work they just did was worth one dollar and that they would have to do the same job over as many times as there were dollars in the bill you just paid.

....

CHAPTER 12

Consistency

Your words are continually educating others around you. Let them create a portrait of enthusiasm and faith.

—TERRY HOGENSON

IF WE ASK OURSELVES WHAT MAKES US FEEL SAFE AND SECURE IN this world, what kinds of answers would we come up with? Things like paying off debt, generating a stable income, steadily increasing a retirement account, and reducing the number of potential financial surprises out there would all come to mind. Each of these answers implies a personal financial commitment that would require a high degree of consistency. Consistent behavior is the only way we can truly attain our financial objectives. Anybody can set a goal, but where the rubber meets the road in financial success is through consistent financial decision making. It only takes a few days of financial irresponsibility to derail a financial plan. Why do you think they put Christmas shopping and New Year's resolutions so close together?

In order for any of us to get anything of substance done over time, we must be able to commit to an objective and then apply ourselves daily toward that objective. This holds true throughout life and is an important part of creating the environment we desire for ourselves and our families. As we develop personal plans and apply ourselves consistently toward their successful implementation, we create habits for ourselves and set examples for our children. These examples will have significant impact on our children's abilities to develop their own personal plans and apply them in their lives.

If our children see us consistently working toward a predetermined objective, they will model their lives after our behavior. Likewise, if they see us spinning about like a ship without a rudder, they will assume that this is an appropriate lifestyle. We must always keep in mind that our level of consistency and the example we set will have a significant impact on our family's life experience and life expectations.

Consistency is vitally important in two areas: household rules and household responsibilities. These areas affect not just the development of our children but ultimately the peace we enjoy in our homes.

Household rules are simply statements of what we can and what we can't do. We need to let our children know, up front, what is appropriate and what's not. When we show them that there is a consistent set of rules to follow, we enable them to negotiate the family landscape without trouble. We must give our children the security of defined boundaries; if we do not, they, and we, will suffer the consequences. Generally, homes that exhibit a higher level of defined behavioral expectations will run more smoothly and turn out more responsible and conscientious young adults than other homes.

Household responsibilities are the things we all do as part of the family. Somebody goes to work to pay the bills, somebody cleans the house and does the laundry, and somebody should make their bed and clean their room, just because they're part of the family. Everyone needs a predefined set of household responsibilities as a member of the family team. By providing responsibilities for them within the home, we enable our children to belong and to be important. They need to know that we depend on them to get

FIGURE 12-1

FAMILY COM-TRACT

Family Motto:_____.

Top Five Household Rules to Remember:

1. _____.
2. _____.
3. _____.
4. _____.
5. _____.

My Two Personal Responsibilities Are:

1. _____.
2. _____.

I will do my best to remember the Household Rules and to take care of my Personal Responsibilities.

_____   _____

Team Member   Date

I will do my best to help my Team Member feel important and needed.

_____   _____

Team Leader   Date

---

their jobs done. They must understand that without their help the home wouldn't run as smoothly and that every family member would be affected.

By establishing household rules and responsibilities, we create a boundary-centered environment that will ultimately enhance our children's abilities to respond properly to different circumstances. When we as parents consistently make sure the rules are followed and responsibilities met, we enable our children to develop self-discipline. With this self-discipline comes a sense of pride, commitment, and personal integrity that will carry them through the challenging times of adult life.

Chapter Challenge ....

Take a moment to sit down with your family and review the Family Com-tract in Figure 12-1. It's called a "Com-tract" because it's all about communicating basic household needs and expectations. In your journal, write down your "Top Five Household Rules to Remember." (Ours are: Homework done before play; respect others property; talk nice; don't leave messes; and in bed on time.) Then write down, for each child, "My Two Personal Responsibilities Are:" and list them. It's important for each child to understand the importance of their commitment and that you are depending on them to uphold what is written in the Com-tract. This information can be found on the KPM.com site as Form CC-12.

....

··

CHAPTER 13

The Family Journal

Enjoy the little things in life, for one day you may look back
and realize that they were big things.

—ANTONIO SMITH

THE FAMILY COM-TRACT MENTIONED IN THE LAST CHAPTER challenge provides us with a great lead-in to this chapter on record keeping. The contract you drew up with your family will go a long way toward establishing a level of order and consistency within your home. There's something about writing everything down that makes things easier to remember and easier to follow. In creating the family com-tract, you have taken the first step in establishing a record-keeping plan for your family.

Detailed record keeping is necessary everywhere in business. No matter what field you are in—education, technology, medicine, aviation (my favorite), or the military—you'll find that a high degree of record keeping is involved. The reason for this is that record keeping enables an organization to function smoothly and efficiently in accordance with its established rules and responsibilities. When you think about it, every record that is maintained has its basis in a rule or a responsibility. By providing detailed documentation that things are done properly and in order, history is created and future progress is promoted.

If we want the future progress and development of our family to be maximized, we'll want to set up some basic record-keeping guidelines for ourselves. Later in this book we discuss some very specific records that we can maintain with our children, but for now we'll stick to the basics.

If you take a moment to review your journal, you'll discover that you've already got a great start to family record keeping.

The basic family records we have discussed are the family contract, the family mission statement, and the family motto. If you've already written these records, congratulations, you're ahead of many of the families out there. If you haven't written these records down yet, stop reading, gather your family (even if it's just you), review chapters 6, 7, and 12, and write down these basic guidelines for yourself.

Now that you've written your family mission statement, family motto, and family contract, you have a set of documents to serve as a foundation for the rest of the records we will be discussing. By defining these three documents early on, everyone in the family knows what's important, what's expected, and where the family is headed. Now let's discuss some of the more specific records you can create to move your family forward, progressing together.

The family journal is an excellent way to keep a record of daily events. The entries to this record don't need to be elaborate or eloquent; they just need to exist. These entries may be as short as a few words ("This day was awesome") or as lengthy as you feel inspired to write; it's up to you and other family members. This record will serve as a bit of a family history and will be cherished as the years roll forward.

As you put your family journal together, even the younger members of your team will have an opportunity to make entries as often as they desire. Some of the most profound writing will come from these little minds. Over the years, the record you create will become priceless as the family grows and changes. You may decide to encourage each family member to keep a separate record for private entries. The family journal will then serve as the public record in which anyone may make an entry. (This includes house-guests and visitors.) The journal will become a fun, exciting, and evolving family storybook, a storybook that will be treasured as a family archive through the years.

Sit down with your teammates and discuss your journal. Make sure that everyone understands that this record is a fun and excit-ing way to express personal feelings about what is happening in the family. You should allow all members of your team to feel free to write anything they wish in the record. Make sure that everyone knows that they should feel comfortable writing anything they want in the record. The journal is about true feelings and atti-tudes. Writing is a terrific form of expression and should be encouraged unconditionally.

Once you have discussed the journal, ask every member to make one small entry to get things started. As the leader of the family, you should go first and write down your feelings about the new journal. You should also write a short bit on each team mem-ber individually. You may wish to address one or more positive attributes you are proud of in that team member and any other feelings that may be appropriate. If you have children that aren't old enough to write yet, tell them that you'll help them make entries until they can write themselves. Tell them what you are writing and what their older siblings are writing, and ask them if you can help them make an entry of their own. By asking what your little ones are thankful for, you'll discover some marvelous family treasures to record.

The family journal provides family members with an opportu-nity to communicate among themselves. It is an excellent place to leave notes and thoughts about what is going on in the family and how you feel. Be sure to mention that the journal isn't an outlet for negative feelings that may develop between family members. Negative feelings are usually only temporary, and the journal represents a permanent record. Even though the negative feelings may be gone, the permanent record remains. If family members have negative thoughts or comments to write, have them use their own personal journals for those feelings.

Keeping a family record may be a little work now, but it will be well worth it later on. Your family journal will be a place to look back on to see how your family has grown and changed over the years. The journal will show where you came from and should pinpoint any defining moments in the lives of your family members. Nothing will be more rewarding to your family than to be able to review the entries made ten, twenty, and thirty years prior. The family journal is like your retirement fund, but instead of saving dollars, you are saving memories.

Chapter Challenge ....

More than likely, you're already off to a great start with your family journal. Open it up and review its contents with your family. Review this chapter and get to work on some of your individual dated entries. Encourage each member to make a first entry as outlined above. Place your journal in a central location where everyone has access to it. At the same time, you may wish to visit a bookstore to review the personal journal section for any family member that may be interested in a more private record. Should your children decide to keep a personal record, they will benefit greatly throughout their emotional development.

··

CHAPTER 14

Financial Intelligence
Overview

Work to become, not to acquire.

—CONFUCIUS

WE'VE GONE OVER A NUMBER OF BASIC FAMILY PRINCIPLES AND have discussed ways in which you, as a parent, can better work with your children in a team environment. This work was necessary in order to create a learning environment conducive to the lessons to be discussed throughout the remainder of this book. If you haven't already done so, I encourage you to go back and accomplish the challenge steps on the family mission statement, family motto, family contract, and family journal. These steps create the communication vehicles and family unity necessary to accomplish the financial lessons outlined throughout the remainder of this book.

Up to this point, you've laid some impressive groundwork. Your team is probably talking a little more freely. You've probably noticed some subtle behavior changes, and you have established the family guidelines necessary to make your children feel safe and secure. Now it's time to look at what you need to do to teach your young teammates about the way they can best develop their personal skills and make the greatest contribution.

The purpose of this book is not to create worldly or materialistic children. Rather, its purpose is to teach children to understand the importance of contribution, effort, and responsibility. We will teach these lessons through a process of goal setting, reward for a quality effort, basic budgeting techniques, and goal attainment to enhance self-esteem. This process has been effective in tens of thousands of homes over the last five years and has enhanced the lives of many young people. It will do the same for your family team and will bring a peace and understanding into your home that you never imagined possible.

The remainder of this book is dedicated to a number of specific financial lessons you can use in your home to teach your children age-specific habits and skills. I'll start out with basic goal setting in order to help get your children emotionally involved in the process. I'll then explain how the kids can look for opportunities to earn and outline several ways for children to take advantage of household opportunities that may exist. After that, I'll talk about behavioral expectations and the possible monetary consequences of breaking the household rules. I'll explain several family record-keeping techniques that will be helpful in teaching these financial lessons as well as other opportunities for family communication.

Step 5, entitled "Saving and Personal Record Keeping," not only discusses helpful record-keeping ideas but reviews basic investment information. I explain the difference between saving and investment, stocks, bonds, and mutual funds, and which type of investing is most appropriate for different investment objectives.

Goal attainment is a special subject that I spend some time on because of its significance in the development of children's self-image and self-esteem. This section has some terrific suggestions and ideas to make goal attainment a special event for your children.

This book was designed to provide you with more than just some guidelines to teach your children money skills. It was designed to be a family focusing instrument that will allow you to create an enhanced family environment. The financial lessons I teach would be significantly less effective if a nurturing, communication-based environment was not present. If you haven't already done so, please review the chapter challenges and implement as many of the suggested family communication techniques as possible.

You will discover that teaching your children financial responsibility can be a fun and rewarding experience for everyone involved. You will grow as a family and will see changes take place almost immediately. The experience of teaching financial skills to your children will be most effective and rewarding if you work on it every day. Your participation is crucial to keeping your children on track and motivated. This system is only as effective as the person teaching it, so get ready, be persistent, and have a good time with the most important people in your life, your family.

Chapter Challenge ....

Gather your family together and review your family mission statement. Discuss what it means and make any enhancements that may be appropriate. Review your family rules and family motto and discuss how having these things can help create family togetherness and enhance communication. Have a family member (the family secretary) record some of the key points that are discussed in the family journal and make note of any positive statements made by family members.

STEP 2
SET YOUR OBJECTIVES

CHAPTER 15

Tired of All Those Toys Lying Around?

The greatest good you can do for another is not just to share your riches, but to reveal to them their own.

—BENJAMIN DISRAELI

BACK IN 1993, I WAS JUST GETTING STARTED IN THE RETAIL brokerage business, and my family was growing. We had two young boys, Jordan, age eight, and Jacob, age four, and things seemed pretty ordinary around the house. Business was going very well and our family income was going up quickly. As our income increased, so too did our propensity to share the wealth with our kids.

When we went to the store to buy a few things, the kids usually tagged along. Invariably, each of the boys would discover a new and exciting trinket that he had to have. We usually bought it for them; doing so was quicker and easier than debating. The kids were proficient deal closers by then, and the items were usually less than five dollars, so at the time it didn't seem like an issue.

As time passed, we began to notice an annoying trend. All of these inexpensive toys were beginning to pile up around the house. The toys were not being taken care of and in many cases were left out, stepped on, and broken. The more toys that were accumulated, the less significant each one became individually. Eventually there came a breaking point.

We were remodeling a couple of rooms in our basement and were expanding the area where the kids normally played. We were doing the work ourselves, and a large dumpster was placed outside our back door for the scrap generated by tearing out the walls. Things were a bit chaotic in the home, but the mess was confined to an isolated area of the downstairs.

One night we had some friends over with their two children. The four boys were downstairs playing and the adults were upstairs talking. As the night progressed, we began to notice an increasing level of noise coming from the basement. When I went down to investigate, I discovered that the kids were having toy wars and were destroying most of the yet-to-be-broken toys in the playroom.

It was upsetting to see such blatant disregard for their possessions and pleasure in the destruction thereof. After viewing the carnage, I just about lost it, but then I quickly regained my composure. I mustered my best, calmest, and deepest parent voice and instructed them to cease toy destruction immediately and pick up the mess. "Yeah, yeah, sure, Dad," was the response. I told them that I was serious and that they needed to get busy and clean up the mess. They said they would.

I wasn't convinced that my message had gotten through and decided to check their progress about ten minutes later. I purposely stepped loudly down the stairs to make sure they knew I was coming and to give them an opportunity to look busy. When I arrived on the scene, I saw that not a toy had been moved and no square inch of floor space was uncluttered. My best and calmest parent voice was failing me. I went louder and deeper and told them, as a drill sergeant tells his troops, that if they didn't get busy and clean the mess up, I was going to take action.

"There, that'll get 'em moving," I thought as I returned to our guests. I figured if I gave them fifteen minutes or so, they would have the room, and their attitudes, straightened out. I waited, we talked, and I listened for cleaning noises from the basement. As the fifteen minutes ticked by, I became more and more angry. The closer the deadline became, the more I realized that they had ignored me, and my drill sergeant voice, for a second time. I again made as much noise as I could walking down the steps. I wanted to give the kids every possible chance to prove themselves good and every possible chance for them to avoid certain destruction.

When I arrived on the scene, it was not a pretty sight. Not a thing had transpired over the last fifteen minutes, and the kids were almost waiting to see what I would do next. I thought, "Now, I'm an educated man. I've served as an officer in the Air Force and have flown numerous military aircraft. I've built a brokerage business from scratch and have surpassed more experienced brokers. I've dealt with about every challenge seen by a man in his mid-twenties, but I'm having a hard time here. I don't know how to get through to these four boys and how to get them to just pick up their toys! Is that so hard? Just pick up your stupid toys!"

The drill sergeant faded and my I'm-about-to-kill-you voice came out. The pointing finger swept the group. "If you don't clean up these toys right now, every one of them is going into the dumpster out back. Now get it done!" I turned and marched back upstairs.

Deep down I knew nothing was going to happen. This was an issue between them and me that went deeper than simple communication. It was an issue based on an overabundance of possessions with no pride of ownership. It was a problem that needed immediate fixing, and I was the right man for the job. As I contemplated my response to what I knew would happen, I decided to begin to throw out some of the broken toys first, to get their attention, and then have a long and meaningful conversation about taking care of what you have and consideration for those less fortunate. It was going to be a powerful educational experience.

Sure enough, when I went to the basement again, nothing had been done. I began to implement my plan. "See, kids, I'm throwing out your toys! Aren't you upset that I'm throwing out your toys? Look at me throwing your beautiful toys in this dirty dumpster! Hey, guys, I'm throwing out your toys here, aren't you devastated?!" They couldn't have cared less. In fact, my youngest, Jacob, actually grabbed some of the toys and began helping me. I was losing it. I couldn't believe what was happening. My kids actually did not care about their toys. All of those items that were so important in the checkout aisle were now meaningless to them. They had no value and the boys had nothing at stake. All they had to do to get those toys was to negotiate properly at the right place and the right time. Something needed to change—not them, but their environment.

From that moment on, my wife and I had a different frame of reference. We understood what happens when children are given everything they want with nothing expected in return. We needed to develop a system that would enable our children to experience what adults in the real world do. Instead of taking the easy road and giving our children what they want, we needed to have them pick an item and set a goal. If our children are influenced to defer gratification and actually earn the dollars necessary to obtain the goal, they will experience the pride of ownership necessary to appreciate and take care of the goal item.

I hope this story illustrates why it is important for you to get involved in your children's financial development. I hope you can learn from this example and that it will motivate you further to get deeply involved in your children's life and financial education.

Over the last six years, since the toy-to-trash experience, I have designed an award-winning children's financial literacy program. The remainder of this book uses various components of this system to help you implement a financial intelligence plan in your own home. You will benefit from our experience over the last several years as I've worked with parents to help them teach their children various financial and life skills. This program requires some effort on your part but is worth it. We've seen the results firsthand and wish now to impress upon you the importance of following through with your plans to give your children financial intelligence.

Chapter Challenge ....

The next time you visit the store with your children and they ask you for something, help them to set the item as a goal. Tell them that if they will do a certain task (something you need done that they can do), you will pay them the money they need to buy the item. It may even be worth it, especially with younger children, to go home and help them to do the job that day, give them a cash payment, and take them back to the store to get the item. By accomplishing these simple steps, you will show your children several key financial principles immediately: goal setting, gratification deferral, opportunity, earning, and spending. This mini-money lesson can be used many times over to reinforce the above-mentioned principles. The more times you conduct a mini-money lesson with your children, the stronger their basic financial skills will become. Document the details of your mini-money lesson in your journal, particularly your children's reaction to the process. Help with your mini-money lesson can be found on KPM.com by printing out Form CC-15.

....

CHAPTER 16

Pride of Ownership

*A mind, once expanded by a new idea, never returns
to its original dimensions.*

—OLIVER WENDELL HOLMES

I MENTIONED IN THE LAST CHAPTER WHY IT'S IMPORTANT TO instill and reinforce a feeling of pride of ownership with your children. It is the pride of ownership that prompts children to take care of their possessions. Without it, things are easily broken, left out, lent to friends, and disregarded. Our job, as parents, must be to make sure our children value what they have and feel the desire to take responsibility for their possessions. We can teach this both by our example as their parents and by their experience within our home.

As the role model in your family, do you set a good example for your children? Do you take pride in your accomplishments and take care of their physical manifestations? Is your home neatly kept and well maintained? Is your car clean and properly serviced? Is your home a place of order and cleanliness? All of these factors significantly contribute to the nurturing environment that is present in your home today. If you sense that there are areas that need improvement, so do your children. Before you can teach pride of ownership, you must manifest it.

One of the reasons that I am able to stay organized, and that my children are highly organized, is that I have had a lot of highly organized examples in my life. My parents were very well organized, both at home and in business. I spent a number of years in the Air Force, and if you want a Ph.D. in organization, you can get it there. I've had the good fortune to have some very well-organized leaders and colleagues in the brokerage business. They helped me set up my business and organize it to produce maximum results. Each of these examples served to solidify the idea that, generally, organization and pride of ownership serve to maximize personal effectiveness. If you make it a point in your life to exhibit personal organization and pride of ownership, your children will see the example necessary to adopt those qualities within themselves.

You can provide your children practical experience in the areas of organization and pride of ownership through the chapter challenge at the end of chapter 15. By enabling children to set a goal and then attain that goal, you will have opened the door to tangible ownership for them. There is no better way for them to experience the principle of ownership than by having to expend personal energy to acquire the funds necessary to obtain an item. Without the effort, ownership means nothing.

Once they actually have attained the goal item, you may find that they will treat that item differently from other possessions they have. When our son Sammy was four, he set his sights on a new Big Wheel. He fed our dog Domino every day for two weeks in order to earn the money necessary to make the acquisition. Grandma found a coupon for five dollars off, and Mom saw that a certain store had them on sale for a limited time. Sammy took his earnings and coupon down to the store with Mom, went to the Big Wheel aisle, picked out his new mode of transportation, and went through the checkout to pay.

That chain of events made a significant impression on Sammy. From the moment he got his new "wheels" home, we saw something special happening. He was careful to take care of it, keep it clean, and put it away when he wasn't using it.

I remember one night, shortly after his new acquisition, his mom and I were putting him to bed. All of a sudden his eyes got big and he started to get up. "What's the matter?" his mother asked.

"I left my Big Wheel outside and I don't want anybody to steal it," was his response.

I don't know of many other young children who have had that experience. At four years of age, this young man had already exhibited the personal characteristics of goal setting, earning, saving, discount pricing, goal attainment, pride of ownership, and responsibility.

Since his first acquisition, Sammy has repeated this formula numerous times for different goal items. Each time he completes his objective and attains his goal item, he strengthens his personal ability and financial intelligence.

Pride of ownership is not something that just happens. Pride of ownership and its companion, organization, come at a price. The price is the experience of setting a goal, working toward the goal, attaining the goal, and taking care of the goal item. After a few times through this process, children will find it to be second nature and will become self-motivated. Once this happens you will find that the parenting challenge becomes smaller and the parenting opportunity becomes greater.

Chapter Challenge ....

Review the details of the mini-money lesson activity from chapter 15. Write down any thoughts you have about the process and its effectiveness. Ask your children about their goal item, if it was worth the work they did, how they feel about the item they picked, and if they think they would like to pick out another item that they can save toward. Write down what happens, and encourage your children to write a brief entry in the family journal about their new item.

....

CHAPTER 17

The Goal Attainment Process (GAP)

Motivation is when your dreams put on work clothes.

—BENJAMIN FRANKLIN

OVER THE LAST COUPLE OF CHAPTERS, I'VE EXPLAINED HOW TO get your kids to focus on some relatively small goal items. Through this experience they have had the opportunity to set a goal, find an opportunity to earn toward the goal, save their money, and then attain the goal item.

This goal attainment process (GAP) is the fundamental cycle of achievement throughout life. Without any one of its components, the GAP fails. Without the goal, there is no motivation and progress is stifled. Without an opportunity, there would be no vehicle to earn and all goals would be unattainable. Without effort applied toward the opportunity, there would be no earnings.

When effort is applied toward the opportunity but no reward is offered, the goal saving progress is eliminated and motivation to apply effort is destroyed. If the earnings are not budgeted properly and are spent and not saved, goal attainment will never occur. If the goal item is removed from the process, saved funds would be redirected somewhere else and the process of earning and saving dollars will lose its focus.

As parents add opportunity and responsibilities into the cycle, children are given the opportunity to experience the effects of their actions in a tangible manner. Once the cycle progresses, parents and children will develop an overall pride in their development process. This pride is important to the overall quality and effectiveness of the experience. While children work their way through the process, a feeling of self-confidence will prevail as goals are achieved and financial experience is gained.

It's important for you to understand each component of the goal attainment process. As you learn the detailed workings of each component, you will gain a greater understanding of how the process will positively benefit your children and your family.

The goal attainment process consists of nine steps:

1. Set goal

2. Provide opportunity to earn

3. Effort to earn (act)

4. Accomplish task (earn)

5. Defer gratification (save)

6. Attain goal

7. Capture experience

8. Build self-esteem

9. Set new goal

A graphic representation of the goal attainment process is shown in Figure 17-1. As shown in the figure, pride in process is central to effective goal attainment and experience capture. As parents provide opportunity and responsibility into the cycle, children gain experience and an increased level of self-confidence.

Figure 17-1   The Goal Attainment Process

I'll spend time discussing each component in greater detail throughout the remainder of this book and guarantee you'll have some great experiences with your family in the process.

The next few chapters will deal with the process of setting goals with your children and making sure you and your kids are working toward the right things at the right time. Children of different ages are capable of different things, as are different types of children. We all know our children intimately and should be able to determine what is appropriate for them at their different stages of development.

The goal-setting process includes a number of different considerations for your family, including the need to start out with a small objective, particularly with younger children. Once your child understands how the GAP works, you may want to increase the size of the goals being attained gradually. Remember, we are trying to expand our children's potential to defer gratification over longer periods of time for more substantial goals.

The older our children, the more appropriate larger goals will become. Once our children possess the skills and discipline, we can begin to discuss multiple goals and integrate a long-term savings program toward a first car or an education. One option you may wish to consider is matching funds toward larger goal items to make them more attainable. Remember, this is an exercise in self-esteem. The greater the accomplishment we can support, the greater the effect on the child. Fund matching is an excellent way to help both.

The final element of the goal-setting process is your example to your children. One of the best ways for you to enhance your example immediately would be through a college savings account for them. Setting one up not only shows them a positive example but also will help reinforce your commitment to them and your self-discipline.

Chapter Challenge ....

The next time you visit the store with your preteen, set a new mini-money lesson goal with your children. Ask them to pick out something small that they would like to have. When you get home, give them a small job or two to earn money toward their new goal. Take them back to the store shortly thereafter and purchase the item with them. Be sure to let your children handle all the money. If you have teen-agers, show them the goal attainment process and ask them if they can explain it to you. They should be able to because they already know everything!

CHAPTER 18

. . . .

Start Out Small

Rivers know this: There is no hurry,
we shall get there some day.

—WINNIE THE POOH

THE SMALLER THE CHILD, THE SMALLER THE GOAL. CHAPTER 15 presented an exercise where a goal was set and attained in one day. This is the most basic example of the goal attainment process we can give our children. They were able to capture the whole process in one quick exercise.

The objective of this book, however, is to extend the time and complexity of the goal attainment process. The ultimate objective is to enable our children to set detailed and well-thought-out goals for themselves, implement a strategic plan for their attainment, and ultimately achieve multiple goals.

The abilities to set goals, defer gratification, and attain goals are skills that will benefit individuals throughout their lifetime. People who possess these skills will have the ability to function at a much higher level than someone who hasn't developed these habits. The more sophisticated people are, the more able they are to postpone gratification in pursuit of an objective.

To analyze this point, consider first the helpless drug addict whose primary driving goal in life is to find a way, any way, to get the next fix. His goal attainment process has a duration of less than one day. The very nature of life for him is immediate desperate action for an immediate, short-duration gratification.

Now let us consider an individual aspiring to be a medical doctor. Here is a person who has set a goal for herself very early in life, possibly in high school or earlier. She's gone through four years of a challenging premed school, four years of medical school, an internship, and residency. This new doctor has deferred gratification for many years in order to attain her goal. Likewise, her life's reward will carry the effect of such planning, preparation, and ability.

These two examples should have impressed upon you the importance of the ability to defer gratification through the goal attainment process. The skills that each person was able to implement in his or her individual life were learned at an early age. The nurturing each received during the early years has manifested itself repeatedly throughout their lives. The parents of the individuals in these examples should share in the credit and the blame for their children's accomplishments and failures.

Chapter Challenge

Review in your mind the goal selection process you have personally chosen. Consider the time commitment you made to your education and the personal goals you have with your career. Are you goal oriented? Do you have a long-term financial plan? What is your personal GAP? Write down any productive thoughts that may come to you during this self-evaluation in your personal journal. Now consider what you have done with your children to help them learn of personal achievement and gratification deferral. "Consider the End!" in all things.

CHAPTER 19

Gradually Increase the Goals

*Everything that enlarges the sphere of human powers, that shows
man he can do what he thought he could not do, is valuable.*

—BEN JOHNSON

THE PRIMARY OBJECTIVE OF THE GOAL ATTAINMENT PROCESS IS
to outline very clearly the path one must choose to get to a predetermined destination. If you understand where you are and where
you want to go and have mapped out a clear course on how to get
there, you've mentally accomplished your objective before beginning. Over time, you have learned how to create this personal road
map to reach your goals. All the events in your life—going
through school, getting a job, starting a business, or raising a family—have provided you with valuable life-planning experience.

As parents, we hope our children will be able to do the same
thing for themselves. Based on our experience and efforts, we can
teach them to define where they are, where they want to go, and
how they can get there. We want to move our children from the
mini-money lesson stage to a point where they are able to clearly
define personal objectives and implement a detailed plan to attain
their goals. If our children possess these skills, they will be able to
create a life for themselves that will be both challenging and
rewarding.

The way we motivate our children to accomplish and succeed is a personal decision. Every child has different capabilities and different skills. One principle that remains constant, however, is the principle of gradual development.

Our children need time to develop, and we shouldn't expect more from them than they are able to do. If we have unrealistic expectations of them, our teaching efforts may have a negative effect and we'll get the opposite of what we're looking for. It is more appropriate to move forward slowly at first with our children than to expect too much too soon. For example, if we started with an item that cost two dollars and took one job to attain the goal, next we may want to find a new goal item that costs four dollars and give children two different job opportunities.

As we slowly move forward with our children, they will catch on to the process and will begin to set higher goals and objectives for themselves. Ultimately, we want our children to motivate themselves, and move forward to larger, more significant items that take more effort, more time, and more planning to achieve. Once they are able to attain large goals through more complex planning and effort, they truly are preparing themselves for an effective and successful life experience.

Chapter Challenge ....

Think about the last mini-money lesson that you conducted. Was it effective? Was it beneficial? Did it make a positive difference in your children? If the answer to any one question is no, try another lesson with a different and more desirable goal item for the children. If the answer is yes to all three questions, help your children pick a new goal item for approximately double the cost and provide two different jobs to complete for the item. Write about your progress and your success in your family journal. Again, Form CC-15 will be helpful in this challenge.

....

CHAPTER 20

Self-Confidence

There is no education like adversity.

—WALT DISNEY

AS OUR CHILDREN GROW IN THEIR ABILITY TO SET LARGER GOALS, they also will grow in their ability to plan out more complicated goal execution strategies. When children realize that they have control over their environment and that they can attain any goal they set for themselves, personal self-confidence will develop naturally. It is this self-confidence that will play a key role in their individual development and will motivate them really to apply themselves and aspire to higher things.

Just like most other personality characteristics, self-confidence is a habit that is developed over time. If children are happy, motivated, and self-confident, most likely they've developed these traits over time through experience. As parents, we have the responsibility and opportunity to instill good habits in our children. The effort-to-reward ratio of this elementary nurturing process is astronomical. While these habits are formed over a relatively short period of time in the home, they will be utilized repeatedly throughout the rest of our children's lives.

As adults, we tend to believe that life is either working collectively for our benefit or conspiring against us. What we believe will depend largely on our past experiences and learned habits. It has been shown that, based on preconceived beliefs, our outcomes will naturally match our expectations. As parents, it is our responsibility to ensure that our children have a high level of self-confidence, only the most positive attitude, and great personal expectations for life.

In developing our children's self-confidence, we must create an environment in our home that is conducive to learning, growth, and understanding. The goal attainment process was designed specifically with this in mind. As we help our children achieve their increasing goals, we are laying the groundwork for a higher level of self-confidence and personal responsibility. As our children grow in these traits, their capacity to self-motivate and accomplish objectives will increase simultaneously.

As parents, we hold our children's future in our hands. If we desire the best for our children, we must determine to foster growth and achievement through a concentrated effort at home. No one else can teach these lessons as effectively as the parent. Remember the Jump$tart survey; close to 90 percent of the respondents said they learned financial (life) skills at home or by themselves. If we want our children to be self-confident and goal-oriented achievers, it is up to us to make it happen.

The following poem was part of a package of Eagle Scout Court of Honor materials from the Boy Scouts of America. It was originally distributed by the Bucks County Council Chapter of the National Eagle Scout Association.

Good Timber

The tree that never had to fight
For sun and sky and air and light,
That stood out in the open plain
And always got its share of rain,
Never became a forest king,
But lived and died a scrubby thing.

The man who never had to toil
Who never had to win his share
Of sun sky and light and air,
Never became a manly man,
But lived and died as he began.

Good timber does not grow in ease.
The stronger wind, the tougher trees,
The farther sky, the greater length,
The more the storm, the more the strength,
By sun and cold, by rain and snows,
In tree or man, good timber grows.

Chapter Challenge ....

Think about a small job that your children can do that may be a little out of their comfort zone. Don't make it too hard, but do make it somewhat challenging for them. Talk to your children about the job and ask them if they could do it to help out. Tell them that you will help them if they get stuck but you want to see them finish the task by themselves. Keep a careful eye on them as they are working and monitor their progress. When they finish, praise them generously for their job and discuss how proud you are of their accomplishment. Ask them how they felt before they started the job, what it felt like when they were doing the job, and how they feel after accomplishing such a big task. Record the answers in your family journal and have your children write a few lines about their experience.

....

CHAPTER 21

Bigger Goals

Treat people as if they were what they ought to be, and you help them to become what they are capable of being.

—Johann Wolfgang von Goethe

So far, we've talked about why goals are important, the goal attainment process, how to start with younger children, and the effect that the goal attainment process has on our children's self-esteem. Most of what we've been covering has been oriented toward younger children. It's important to start the financial education process as early as possible, preferably between the ages of four and nine; however, children of any age will benefit from being introduced to the process.

The key to getting the attention of older children, between ages eleven and fifteen, is the same as that of their younger siblings: the goal. The goals they set for themselves will determine their level of excitement and determination toward goal attainment. If you try to set their goal for them, don't be surprised to find them less than enthusiastic about the whole thing.

If, on the other hand, they have been given the opportunity to pick whatever they want, you'll see a whole different level of commitment in the process.

For the younger kids, I suggested to keep the goal items smaller and more attainable. If children have been working with the system for a while, they may be ready for a larger challenge. They will let you know when this happens. Likewise, older kids may want to start out with something a little more challenging. Musical instruments have been the most popular goal item for our thirteen-year-old, Justin.

About three years ago, when Justin was ten, we introduced him to our new program. Initially he wasn't that enthused; after all, he had been getting a free ride with allowance for quite a while. But once he started talking about his interest in music, particularly drums, we had the hook we needed.

Shortly thereafter, we took him down to our local music store and let him browse around for a while. We could tell he was excited, and we even had the store manager help him sit down and pound out a few beats. We had Justin pick out a starter set and take a brochure with a picture. After he put the picture in his room to remind him of his goal, he was ready to go. At this point, he was sufficiently motivated to take advantage of the opportunities we would provide for him.

To add fuel to the fire, we decided that we would match any dollars that he earned by working around the house. This is a good idea, especially for larger goal items that might ordinarily be out of reach for the earner. The larger the goal attained, the greater the effect on self-confidence and self-esteem. By making the goal that much more attainable, we were helping Justin move very quickly toward goal attainment and increasing his level of commitment to the process.

After the visit to the music store, we were amazed at his level of participation in the events around the house. He was determined to accomplish his objective and was constantly looking for ways to help out and earn toward his drum set. We all had our daily responsibilities around the house, and those had to be done before any opportunity jobs were started. In other words, we still expected him to participate in his personal responsibilities as a member of the family.

A good rule of thumb that we've used to differentiate between money jobs and family jobs is personal hygiene. If the job has anything to do with our personal space or appearance, we do it because we live in the home. Examples may be to make your bed or clean your room, take a shower, and brush your teeth. Each of these jobs must be done daily before any earning can take place.

With a clearly defined objective, rules of the game in place, and plenty of opportunity to earn, Justin was strongly positioned to experience personal success. We encouraged him and praised him for his determination, and within two months, he had earned enough to purchase his objective.

We made sure that he had his cash ready and then took him to buy his drums. It was probably one of the most memorable events in his life, and he was totally motivated as a result of the experience. When we got home, we set up the drum set and let him go at it. He played for four hours straight.

As a result of his goal attainment process, Justin valued his drums more than if they were merely purchased for him. From the first day out of the boxes, he spent time practicing and working on his talent. It wasn't very long before he decided he wanted to be in the school band; soon after that he attained first chair. He was motivated because of the experience, and he was dedicated to getting the most out of his purchase.

Since that time his skills have grown tremendously, and teachers and other students have regularly requested that he help with various productions put on by the school. His talent is now well known and he is sought out. I'm sure you can imagine what his self-image and self-confidence are like.

As you work with your older children, let them pick the area in which they want to excel. They know better than anyone what is going to motivate them. If they want goofy clothes, let them get goofy clothes. It's not the item that is important, it's the experience of getting there. Once you've established your determination to help your children attain their goals, you'll be helping them acquire life skills that will benefit them throughout their lives. They'll not only be determined to reach objectives that they set for themselves, but they will carry the feelings of self-worth and self-confidence throughout the process.

Chapter Challenge ....

Talk with your children about what interests them. Ask questions such as these:

What did you do today?

What was the best thing about your day today?

If we could go and do anything at all right now, what would you like to do?

What's the funniest thing you've ever done?

If you could have anything in the world, what would it be?

The answers to these questions will provide an opportunity for you to ask more detailed queries. The purpose of this exercise is to uncover a core motivation for your children. Whatever that motivation may be, you'll want to work with them in that area. If you find that a particular motivational area is risky or unacceptable, you may need to suggest an alternative, safer option. To create an alternative motivation, you may have to expose them to new activities. Have you gone fishing? Flown a kite? Built a model together? Gone shopping? Gone for a bike ride? Played a game of Horse? Drawn a picture? Listened to some music? Read a story? Read the paper? Watched the news? Gone hiking? Each of these activities will give you subtle clues as to your children's areas of interest. When you uncover something that really excites your children, give them an opportunity to set a goal in that area. Have them think about what it would be like to accomplish the objective, and let them know that you will help them attain their goal.

. . . .

CHAPTER 22

Life-Planning Workshop

*Persistence. Nothing in the world can take the place of
persistence. Talent will not; nothing is more common than
unsuccessful men with talent. Genius will not; unrewarded
genius is almost a proverb. Education will not; the world is
full of educated derelicts. Persistence and determination
alone are omnipotent. The slogan, "Press on," has solved
and always will solve the problems of the human race.*

—CALVIN COOLIDGE

BEING THEIR OWN BOSS IS THE ULTIMATE OBJECTIVE OF MOST PEOPLE
in the workforce today. To some extent, we all want to have control
over our own destiny and to be able to make a difference in the
world. This objective is universal, but few realize that they have the
power within themselves to accomplish that objective.

If you are working for someone, you have the opportunity to be
your own boss immediately. I don't mean you should go out and
quit your job. The fact is, you probably feel and act as if you are
accountable to your employer or your immediate supervisor. You
do things out of obligation or necessity. But, if you think about it,
your first accountability is to yourself. If you hold yourself to a
higher standard than anyone else ever could, you'll automatically
become your own boss.

One of the most common characteristics among successful

entrepreneurs and business professionals is that they hold themselves to a higher degree of accountability. By doing so, they continually challenge themselves and ensure that they perform at an optimal level. As they operate at these extraordinary levels, they add a tremendous amount of value to their organization.

This type of self-discipline and commitment is necessary to achieve the highest potential in life. The only difference between people's success or mediocrity in any given endeavor is the level to which they commit to a task and apply themselves. Just as with our children's goal attainment, we must apply ourselves diligently to our own personal success. If you see the parallels between a successful adult experience and what I've been discussing for your children, you're beginning to get the picture.

Whether you're a corporate executive or an hourly employee, the principles of commitment apply to you. If you make the choice to hold yourself to a higher level, everyone you are in contact with will recognize and benefit from your efforts. The increased self-confidence and pride you will feel will be a catalyst for future achievement and advancement. The example you set for your children will be noticed and emulated. Your quality of life will improve, and opportunities will open up from places you never imagined possible.

As you make the commitment to hold yourself to a higher level, share the experience with your family. Talk about the ways in which you intend to create greater value in your profession. Include your children in some of your personal brainstorming sessions to figure out better ways of accomplishing your objectives. Let them see how committed you are to achieving personal goals. Also let them see how committed you are to creating a better environment around your home. Discuss ways in which you can participate in the family that will enhance the environment for the benefit of all family members. Hold yourself accountable to your position within your family, and expect more out of yourself than any other family member ever could.

This same attitude of drive, excitement, and motivation is what we wish for our children. By setting an example for them to follow, we will multiply the results of our parenting efforts dramatically. We all know that "do as I do" is much more effective than "do as I say." By making a personal commitment in your own profession, the example you set will add volumes to the educational process that is taking place in your own home.

The principles I have been discussing thus far are universal. By encouraging your children to attain the goals they have set for themselves while at the same time sharing your experience in your own goal attainment process, you will create a lasting impression that will have an extraordinary effect on your entire family. By working together to become better family members, sharing personal experiences, and ultimately striving to be contributing members of society, you lay the foundation for personal success, happiness, and achievement.

Chapter Challenge ....

Have a brainstorming session with yourself, and try to think of ways in which you could improve your work environment. In what ways could you make a greater contribution? How could you add value to your position within your organization? Put together a list of three things that you could do immediately to enhance your position. Write these things down and commit to applying them over the next thirty days. Likewise, sit down with your family and discuss ways in which each member could add value to the family equation. Have each family member write down one objective in the family journal, and commit to it for the next thirty days. Share your experiences with one another as you begin to feel the positive effects of your new level of commitment.
....

LOOK FOR OPPORTUNITY

CHAPTER 23

Family Jobs

No other success can compensate
for failure in the home.

—DAVID O. MCKAY

IN OUR HOUSE THERE ARE TWO DIFFERENT KINDS OF JOBS, family jobs and opportunity jobs. Family jobs are the things we do because we live in the house (we'll discuss opportunity jobs in the next chapter). Our kids know that, each day, they have to make their beds and clean their rooms before they do anything else. They also know that they need to take a shower once in a while and keep their teeth semi-white. These family jobs are expected in exchange for all of the other great benefits of living in our home: free food, free shelter, cable television, and the opportunity to have great parental examples.

Part of our family mission statement says that we will all pitch in and do our fair share of the household work. We sat down with our children early on and defined for them what was expected. This was easy because we simply made our children accountable for their own personal space. The younger ones were taught how to make their beds and put their toys away; the older ones were expected to do the same but were given additional responsibilities. The older the children got, the greater their household responsibilities. As the kids reached their teens, we even had them doing their own laundry and supervising their younger siblings.

We have been very fortunate and have had a relatively easy time getting our kids to participate in the family job responsibilities. You probably will be as successful if you clearly define all children's participation and help them to understand how valuable they are to the family unit. If they feel that the rest of the family is depending on them, they will want to do a good job and keep things running smoothly. Children need to be safe, but they also need to feel needed. Rather than making daily family responsibilities into chores that the children have to do, explain the overall benefits that accrue to the family as a result of their participation. By doing so, you will change the way your children feel about being in the family as well as the way they feel about themselves.

Family jobs provide a good opportunity for children to learn about taking care of themselves. Remember hearing about the young college freshman getting to campus and dealing for the first time with laundry, cooking, and finance? As parents, we have the opportunity to prepare our children to address these real issues while they are still in the home. The one life transition that is usually quite abrupt is when kids move out of the home and are confronted for the first time with real-world issues. If they already have done their own laundry or cooked their own meals and made their own beds and balanced a checkbook, they can focus on the challenges of college or that first job instead of being overwhelmed with basic life skills implementation.

Once you've established the family jobs for your children, you'll want to think about what they can do to help out around the house to earn a little income. Cooking, cleaning, dishes, laundry, pets, auto maintenance, and yard work all provide parents with plenty to do after a hard day's work. In the next chapter I'll discuss how many of these jobs can be turned into an opportunity to earn for your young learners.

Chapter Challenge ....

Sit down with your family and write down a list of all the jobs that are done in the home by everyone over one week. This list should include everything from brushing teeth every night to cleaning the garage on Saturday morning. As you think about what gets done in your home, you'll be surprised at the number of weekly tasks. Don't leave anything out. If you vacuum, dust, feed a pet, walk a pet, sweep a floor, or fold a towel, write it down. The idea here is for your kids to get an idea of what really happens in the home throughout a week. Let them understand that the home isn't on autopilot and that somebody—usually you—has to do this stuff. KPM.com Form CC-23 will be helpful here.

Once you're done with the list, have your children pick out the jobs that they think they could do to help out. Assign their name to only one or two of the listed jobs, and have them accomplish those tasks during the upcoming week. Once an appropriate number of family jobs have been assigned, this sheet becomes your weekly family jobs summary. In most families, having the children make their beds and clean their rooms in the morning will constitute the bulk of their family job responsibilities. The younger the child, the lower the percentage of the total weekly workload they should be expected to do. You'll probably want the younger kids to be responsible for only their own room at the start. As kids reach their teen years, they should feel as if they have an age-appropriate level of responsibility around the house. By the time they are ready to leave the home, they should be able to participate in the home at an adult level and truly should be ready to take care of themselves in the real world.

After you've decided who can do what, and have completed your weekly summary, post this agreement in the family journal and have everybody sign it. When it's in writing, you will have a record to review if questions develop.

Have your children check off their responsibilities as they are completed. Depending on how well the children acclimate to their responsibilities, you may want to move jobs around from time to time. Each week, review the family jobs that are getting done, and make sure your children keep a positive team spirit as things get done. Usually if you're happy in helping them, they'll be happy in return.

. . . .

CHAPTER 24

The Earnings Evolution

Lack of money is no obstacle. Lack of an idea is an obstacle.

—ANONYMOUS

ONCE YOU'VE ESTABLISHED WHAT NEEDS TO BE ACCOMPLISHED around the house and everybody is pitching in to get the jobs done, you'll be ready to talk about additional ways for your children to earn. How to earn money is one of the most basic issues faced by adults on entering the workforce. However, most adults cannot tell you where they learned about earning. Even though this skill is one of the most critical, acquiring it is largely left to chance.

Teaching our children how to earn is an important role that we, as parents, must play. By having the opportunity to earn for themselves, our children's self-esteem and self-confidence can be greatly enhanced. By experiencing the benefits of earning at an early age, our children can gain a valuable insight into the principles of real-world economics. In gaining this insight, they will obtain the practical earnings experience they need before being launched out on their own.

Typically, children learn about earning only by accident, when they are introduced to their first job. This may be through a friend or relative during high school. Given the importance and long-term implications that these earning skills will have in an individual's life, it would be more appropriate for children to learn about earning at an early age in a structured environment. As I've already mentioned, this environment is best established in the home through the opportunities we can create for our children.

Obtaining an awareness of basic financial literacy is a building process. Principles such as goal setting and earning must be understood. Our children need to comprehend the basics of effort and reward before they will be ready to learn more sophisticated financial principles such as saving, budgeting, borrowing, and interest.

Giving our children the opportunity to earn an income by participating in the housework is the first step toward creating this financial awareness. We as adults value what we have because of the effort it took to earn the dollars we used to obtain goods or services. Likewise, our children can experience this value through generating earnings of their own.

As previously mentioned, there are two categories of household jobs, family jobs and opportunity jobs. Family jobs are those things that we do because we are part of a family. These jobs may include making our bed or keeping our room clean. Opportunity jobs are tasks that can be done by our children to reduce our parental home workload. These jobs may include tasks such as vacuuming the carpets, mowing the lawn, or doing the dishes. In the last chapter, you listed many of the household jobs that needed to get done throughout the week. If you're like me, most of the jobs fall under the responsibility of the parent, with a few select jobs going to the kids as family jobs.

Through opportunity jobs, we as parents can easily establish a way for our children to create an income for themselves. By posting a list of opportunity jobs in the home, we provide our children the chance to make as much or as little as they want. A posted chance to earn creates a lesson in one of life's greatest motivators, the opportunity to seize the day through a personal choice to make the most of it.

In offering income opportunities to our children, we may want to establish some quality control guidelines as well. Doing so will ensure that our kids understand that it's not enough just to get the job done, it must be done properly. A simple way to do this is to create a quality scale for job accomplishment, for example, 50% payment for a job done halfway. We'll discuss this in greater detail in the next chapter.

Children of different ages are capable of accomplishing different things. I like to say that the older the child is, the farther away from the kitchen they can work. To illustrate this point, I have created an earnings evolution of different jobs for different ages:

Job	Age
Feed pets	4–8
Set and clear table	5–9
Water plants	6–8
Vacuum and dust	7–12
Dishes and laundry	8–18
Clean garage	9–18
Mow lawn, shovel driveway	10–18
Mow lawn, shovel driveway (neighbors')	12–18
Paper route	13–18
Golf caddie	14–18
Fast food, retail sales	16+

As you can see, the older the children are, the farther away from the safety of the home they can venture. This process will continue throughout life with college, graduate school, and different employment opportunities.

Another way to create earnings for school-age children is to include academic accomplishment as an earnings opportunity.

Good grades are the children's job while in school; why not reward them for it? You also might want to encourage certain habits or behaviors by offering a reward for action. We've done this with reading for our own children.

Reading is an important element of intellectual development. If you want your children to excel academically, you'll want them to be good readers when they start. One way that we have helped our kids become good readers is to get them in the habit of reading regularly.

Forcing our children to read for a certain amount of time every day would have been highly ineffective. They would have done it out of respect for us, but the motivation would have been based on negative reinforcement rather than positive initiative. Instead, we decided to reward our children with a certain dollar amount for every twenty minutes that they read. We also established the household rule that they needed to be in bed by a certain time. They didn't have to be asleep, just in bed.

What happened was just what we wanted: The kids were in bed on time and reading. Each had his own preference and each developed a desire to share with us what he was reading about. After about three months, the habits of going to bed at a certain time and reading good books were reinforced simultaneously.

Now, because of the earnings opportunity we associated with reading years ago, our children have become exceptional readers. We don't pay them to read anymore; they do it because they've learned how much enjoyment comes from the experience. They also go to bed about the same time every night—not because of any demand we impose but because of the habit established years earlier.

As parents, we can provide opportunity to our children in a number of ways. Each family is different, and each child is capable of different tasks. It's always important to remember that some things are done because you are a member of the family. If our family has a "yard day" on Saturday morning, for example, the kids know that it's time to pitch in and get some work done. On the other hand, if one child is saving hard for something, we may decide to create an extra opportunity or two to help him reach his goal.

Chapter Challenge ....

Sit down with your children and discuss the most recent goal item that they have selected for themselves. Talk about how quickly they think they will be able to get to their goal and what kind of jobs they are doing to earn income toward the goal. Consider the earnings evolution as well as a new desirable behavioral characteristic you would like to see in your children. Come up with two additional opportunities for them to earn income toward their goals.

....

···

CHAPTER 25

What's It Worth?

While one person hesitates because he feels inferior, another is busy making mistakes and becoming superior.

—HENRY C. LINK

IN CHAPTER 23 I TALKED ABOUT THE IMPORTANCE OF FAMILY jobs and helping your children understand the necessity of their role in the family team. Then in chapter 24 I discussed how to help your kids attain their goals through opportunity jobs and by creating an earning environment in your home. In this chapter I'll touch briefly on how to help your children understand the negotiation process in determining what each opportunity job might be worth.

Knowing how to negotiate is an essential skill for any adult, whether in business, while buying a car, or simply within the family environment. In the United States, negotiating is not admired and we have lost a great deal of our negotiating skills. When we go to the store, we don't have to barter or squabble with the cashier; we know the prices are "set" and that there's not much we can do about it. The only time most adults get into a negotiation about price is at the car lot, and because of our lack of negotiation experience, we usually walk out with less than the ideal deal, and we feel that way.

The art of negotiation must be learned. It ties in a great deal with our communication and expression skills. If people are good negotiators, it's probably because their parents were good negotiators and the personal communication levels were high in their homes. If they are poor negotiators, it is likely because they had little opportunity to negotiate or express themselves while growing up. If this is the case, family communication levels may have been limited and children's communication, self-expression, and negotiation skills have suffered.

As parents, we have the opportunity to help our children become great expressors, negotiators, and communicators. One of our primary responsibilities is to help our children acquire these necessary communication skills. Without the ability to negotiate, communicate, and express, our children will suffer the consequences and frustration that accompany a lack of talent in these areas.

Our children will gain valuable experience through many of the techniques discussed in this book. The chapter challenges are largely communication-based exercises aimed at breaking through personal and intrafamily communication barriers. This section deals specifically with the negotiating element of the communication process. By allowing your children to place a value on their work and express that value to you, they gain essential self-expression experience.

Children need to feel that their efforts are acknowledged and worthy of reward. By placing a specific value on a task successfully completed, children gain a tangible sense of the value of their efforts. The greater they believe their reward should be, the greater their self-estimation. The greater their self-estimation, the greater their ability to contribute positively to their environment. The greater their ability to contribute, the more personal power they will possess to make a positive difference throughout their lives.

Once our children feel that they are able to exchange their efforts for a worthwhile reward, they have the necessary tools to clearly map out a path between where they are and where they want to go (their goal). By establishing a clear path to goal attainment, children have an unencumbered opportunity to get what they want as quickly as they want it. The ability to set, map, and attain goals is key to life planning and the cornerstone of personal motivation. Self-esteem comes from the ability to place a value on one's contribution, communicate that value to another, and then have that value independently affirmed. By repeating this process often, the skills of communication, self-expression, and negotiation are greatly enhanced. A young adult equipped with these skills will possess a great advantage over contemporaries when faced with real-world issues.

The need to be accountable for the quality of work done balances self-expression, communication, and negotiation. If we possess a high self-esteem but deliver low-quality work, an imbalance exists. Individuals who have high self-esteem and demand a high reward for their efforts must be accountable to that demanded reward. When we instill this expectation in our children, they will develop the ability to articulate self-value plus a pride in accomplishment that will manifest itself in the form of a quality job done.

One way to address the issue of a quality job done is in the form of a quality scale for work. For example, if an opportunity to clean the garage was posted for $5 and the job was only 50% percent done, the reward would be only $2.50. Likewise, if the same job were done extraordinarily well with a high degree of care, then the reward may be $6 or $7. We want to encourage a best effort and reward accordingly.

Isn't this what happens to us in our own endeavors? If we are conscientious in our efforts and always strive to do our best, aren't we rewarded accordingly? Not just with money, but doesn't our self-confidence and pride increase? Don't we carry that feeling of pride and accomplishment forward to other tasks and situations? It is this feeling that serves to motivate us and drive us to higher levels of accomplishment in both work and family. This cycle of higher and higher achievement ultimately propels us toward our own personal self-actualization.

Once we have experienced these feelings of pride and accomplishment, we want to share the feelings with those we care about, particularly our own children. As we teach these principles to them, we ourselves become stronger and more motivated in our efforts.

By introducing our children to the basic elements of this cycle—self-expression, communication, negotiation, and accountability—we provide them with the foundation necessary for personal achievement. Ultimately, what we wish to effect in our children is a combination of an appropriate level of self-esteem and a high degree of pride in their work. This winning combination will serve your children throughout their lifetime and will benefit all those who come into contact with them.

Chapter Challenge ....

Review the two new jobs assigned through the last chapter challenge. Ask what the tasks or accomplishments ought to be worth if done completely. Allow your children to express their self-estimation, then clearly define what you would expect to constitute a completed job. Review the quality scale idea and have your children perform each job. Work with them during the process and continually encourage them to make an extra effort. See that the jobs are completely done and help children exceed your quality expectations. After you're done working together, sit down and explain that their effort and the job quality were extraordinary. Reward the effort with an amount that exceeds what was agreed upon. Share the achievement publicly and build up the accomplishment with other family members. Write about the experience in your family journal and have your children do the same.

....

CHAPTER 26

Effort and Reward

*Far and away the best price that life has to offer is the chance
to work hard at work worth doing.*

—Theodore Roosevelt

One of the best ways for you to put the lessons we've been discussing into a proper perspective for your kids is to let them experience what you do all day long. By showing them what you do every day, you give them a good picture of what they may confront as adults. This is an excellent opportunity to share what you've learned with your children.

We have been working with your children to teach them about setting goals and looking for opportunity to earn income toward their goal attainment. As your children learn to earn, they will begin to understand the relationship between effort and reward. As their experience grows, they will begin to have an interest in what you do for a living and how much you make for your effort. Undoubtedly they have observed how hard you work and have a good understanding of what those earnings can provide for the family.

As your children begin to ask questions about your job, your income, and how these two elements work together, you may want to sit down and show them how effort and reward works for you.

You can do a couple of things to help them gain an understanding of how your real world works. One would be to take your young children to work with you for a few hours. The other may be to review your paycheck with them and explain the various deductions. Ideally, you'll want to do both so they can get the complete picture.

You may decide to go in on a Saturday morning and simply show the kids around the workplace, talk about what you do, and let them know how you feel about your job and what your aspirations are. Highlight any initiatives you may have taken to improve your position, and impress upon them the importance of doing their best at all times.

If you've decided to show your paycheck to your children, make sure that they know that this is private. Let them know that it would be inappropriate for them to talk to anyone about the experience. They need to understand that it wouldn't be polite to brag about how much you make and how "rich" you are.

When you discuss your paycheck, make sure you talk about each deduction and review what each means. Talk about your taxes, and let your children know how taxes help maintain schools and roads and help to keep the country safe. It's important to be positive and to avoid any disparaging remarks or negative political opinions about our government. Children will have plenty of time to determine their own political opinions.

If you are contributing to a retirement plan, show your children how the account has grown and explain what the retirement vehicle is for. You need not disclose exact balances if you're not comfortable doing so, but it's important for your children to understand the importance of saving and investment. Knowing that you're putting money away for the future will add significantly to their level of security in the home.

You've got a great opportunity to share some financial information with your children. They will benefit from their new understanding gained through your teaching efforts. By putting effort and reward into a proper perspective for your children, you enable them to appreciate the household money lessons that you are teaching them. Just think about how your perspective may have been changed if your parents had taken the time to do these exercises with you when you were your children's age.

Chapter Challenge ....

You guessed it! Try to arrange a special visit to your workplace with your children. Let them see what you do, and explain how you were able to attain the position you have. Share with them details about your earnings, and help them to understand your personal effort and reward equation. Explain the impact of taxes, and talk about any retirement plan contributions. Review any retirement plan statements you may have, and show them the importance of an investment accumulation. Write any positive or humorous remarks in your family journal, and let your children enter their impressions as well.

....

CHAPTER 27

A Job or a Career?

Make the most of yourself, for that is all there is for you.
—RALPH WALDO EMERSON

AS YOU'VE BEEN WORKING WITH YOUR CHILDREN, THEY HAVE HAD a chance to observe what you do, how you do it, and how hard or easy your job may be. They've also had the chance to gain some insight regarding the financial benefits derived from such an occupation. They are beginning to understand that what you do is different from what other adults do and that different occupations offer various levels of compensation.

As your children grow in their understanding of how the effort-to-reward equation works, eventually they will come to a point where they should be shown the difference between a "job" and a "career." Contrary to what you may be thinking right now, the difference between a job and a career has nothing to do with income but everything to do with attitude. Any occupation can be a job and any occupation can be a career; it depends on the level of commitment applied.

I've known many executives who have a respectable position in a strong company but lack commensurate commitment and professionalism. These executives only have jobs. Likewise, I've known young individuals earning minimum wage who pour their hearts and souls into an opportunity to make a difference. These young achievers are starting their professional careers. The difference between a job and a career is the level of commitment and professionalism exhibited by the earner. One is destined for greatness and the other for mediocrity; you know which one is which.

As a parent, it's your responsibility to teach your children the importance of picking a career over a job. They need to be able to identify an earnings opportunity and commit their best efforts in task accomplishment. By taking a high degree of pride in their work, even if it's just feeding the dog, they are taking their first steps toward a fulfilling and satisfying life experience.

Your children will grow and mature in their ability to set goals, earn, and save. They will recognize the differences between careers and will begin to comprehend that different efforts offer different rewards. Now, there's no magic formula that will guarantee an optimal financial reward for effort, but there is one common denominator in the effort-to-reward equation, and that is specialized knowledge through education.

With the exception of the entrepreneur, education plays the most significant role in determining compensation and opportunity available for entry-level employees. According to 1997 Census Bureau figures, the gap in average annual earnings by education level is on the rise. An individual without a high school diploma earned only $16,124 annually. The high school graduate earned an average $22,895 per year. The bachelor's degree holder earned an average of $40,478, and the advanced degree holder earned an impressive $63,229 per year.

If you average this over thirty years of employment, the high school graduate will earn $203,130 more than a friend who quit school in tenth grade. The bachelor's degree holder will earn $527,490 more than the high school graduate, and the advanced degree holder will earn $682,530 more than the bachelor's degree holder. If children decide not to quit school in tenth grade and continue to go to school through an advanced degree, that decision will be worth an average of $1,413,150. I hope this number means something and provides children with sufficient motivation to study hard and stay in school.

A positive attitude and personal commitment will affect every area of life including work, education, relationships, and service. By helping your children understand and adopt these principles early, you'll go far to ensure their future success. Show them how, by their staying in school an extra six years (only six years), they stand to earn literally millions of dollars more over a lifetime. Figure 27-1 depicts lifetime earnings by education level.

FIGURE 27-1   Average Lifetime Earnings (30 Years)

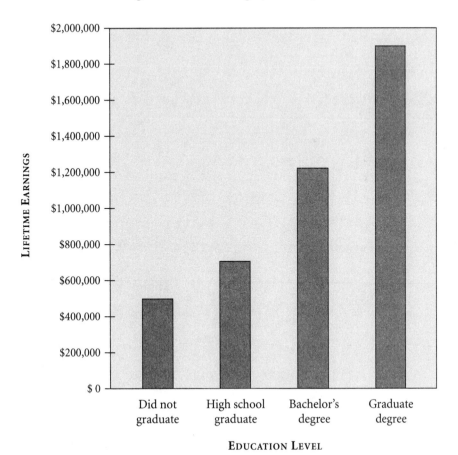

Chapter Challenge ....

Review the education figures with your children, and help them to understand the difference between a job and a career. Explain the income figures in terms they can comprehend. As an example, $1,413,150 is 282,630 Beanie Babies, 11,776 BMX bikes, or 23,951 new Nintendo games. Have them write their impressions in the family journal.

....

CHAPTER 28

Encouraging the Learntrepreneur

The future belongs to those who believe
in the beauty of their dreams.

—ELEANOR ROOSEVELT

IF YOU TAKE A LOOK AROUND, YOU'LL SEE THAT MANY TIMES children will choose an occupation similar to that of their parents. Children of doctors feel comfortable looking for a career in medicine. Accountants usually give birth to little future accountants. Stockbrokers usually encourage their young ones to choose a career in the financial services industry; after all, it is the greatest business in the world!

As adults, we are comfortable encouraging our children to do as we have done. There is nothing we know better than our own experiences, and we would like nothing better than to provide our children with the same opportunity. This transgenerational flow of occupational information is great, as long as our children don't have other talents or desires that would be conducive to success in another area.

For instance, our son Justin is an extraordinary musician at the age of thirteen after only a few formal lessons and only a couple of years with his instruments. He has exhibited a desire to learn and practice on his own, so his mother and I have made the determination to support him all we can. We have given him the opportunity to earn and quickly save for any additional equipment he needs for his music. As a result, he now writes his own music on the computer and plays it on the guitar, keyboard, and drums. He also records individual tracks and mixes the music himself. While he won't be in an occupation as great as the financial services industry like his dad, he's doing what he wants and is quickly developing more than anyone has ever seen, including his instructors.

We can help our children discover their own talents and desires while they're still within the protective walls of their own home. When most adults come into contact with young children, one of the first questions asked is: So what do you want to do when you grow up? This is because most adults still don't know the answer themselves! Their parents never took the time to help them understand the importance of self-direction, decision, and commitment.

I grew up in a fairly typical family and was left to discover many of life's little secrets on my own. There was no free ride, and I was encouraged early on to be independent and accountable for my decisions. If I wanted to go to college, this was something I needed to figure out for myself. (By the way, I wouldn't recommend this to other parents, it made getting an education unnecessarily difficult.) Because I was given the opportunity to be self-directed, I chose a course that offered the most flexibility and opportunity for growth.

I spent a number of years in the Air Force and then spent an equal number of years in the retail brokerage business. Both experiences were meaningful to me, and both provided opportunities for personal growth and development. But it wasn't until I started my own company that I felt truly fulfilled. I left the brokerage business over three years ago to start Cash University, a company dedicated to teaching young people money management skills.

Even though I have never made more than one-quarter the income that I did as a broker (that's right, only 25%), I still get more personal gratification from the experience. I probably work at more than twice the intensity and number of hours (it's 1:30 A.M. as I write this), yet I feel much more fulfilled. Maybe it's because the company and its products came from inside my head, maybe it's because I'm helping kids gain a better financial insight, or maybe it's because all the hard work has fried the better portion of my brain and I don't know any better; I can't explain it. Whatever it may be, I like being an entrepreneur and the challenges it places on the body, mind, and soul.

As I see my children grow, I can't help but think about their career decisions and what might interest them. Each of the boys is different. They have different interests, different capabilities, and different desires. The one thing that I would like to expose each one to, however, is the opportunity to create their own enterprise, to help them, at least once in their lives, to start something of their own, develop it, run it, and finish it.

When children are young, this is fairly easy. If you remember the earnings evolution, there came a point around age twelve when they first started working away from home (shoveling neighbors' driveways, mowing lawns). It's about this time that they are old enough to experience the effort-to-reward equation with OPM. (other people's money). Once they start working for OPM, their working experience, responsibility, and the job pride they established at home will come into play. It's at this point that you'll discover that your financial intelligence efforts were definitely worthwhile. If your neighbors call to compliment you on how great your earner is, congratulations; if they call to have you come and pick up your kid, better plan on some more homework on the GAP.

As your children hit twelve years of age or older, you may want to help them set up their own little enterprise. Some children will want to do this on their own without any prompting, while others will need a little encouragement to get started. Either way, discovering the positive feelings associated with managing their own project is a good experience for them.

Some of the projects that we have seen over the years are a lemonade stand, a car wash, a pet photo shop, a garage sale management service, a pet grooming service, a lawn mowing service, a snow shoveling service, and most recently an Internet site design service. Each of these entrepreneurial ventures provides a varying degree of opportunity, complexity, and time commitment. Each will provide an excellent opportunity for children to discover what it's like to be a learntrepreneur.

An essential step for your learntrepreneur to get started is to help them put together a brief business plan. Included in this will be a statement of purpose (why are you doing it), a summary of the materials needed, a plan to accomplish the purpose, and a statement of the desired outcome. The plan doesn't need to be very long, but it does need to be specific and complete.

Figure 28-1 will give you and your learntrepreneur an excellent template to review while considering a new enterprise. For your convenience, you can go to KPM.com and print out a copy of Form MBP-1.

By considering the enterprise and evaluating it through the listed questions, you'll be well on your way to helping your learntrepreneurs figure out how to accomplish their objectives.

Initially, you'll want to keep close tabs on project development. Make sure your learntrepreneur is following their plan and staying on budget. Help them as much as they will let you, and provide loads of verbal support and encouragement. Once you see that they've got it under control, let them take total charge and run with the plan. You'll be amazed at what this experience can do for your young learntrepreneur and the effect it will have on their personal outlook on life.

While your children may not get totally excited about the project, they will definitely remember it for the rest of their lives. The

Figure 28-1

MINI–BUSINESS PLAN OUTLINE GUIDE

"If you choose a job you love, you'll never have to work another day in your life."

—Confucius

1. What do you enjoy doing (i.e., 1. being outdoors, 2. spending time with animals, 3. riding my bike)?_____

   _____

2. How could you incorporate that in your business (i.e., 1. lawn service, 2. pet service, 3. paper route)?_____

   _____

3. Who are your prospective customers?

   _____

   _____

4. What materials will you need (i.e., lawn mover, supplies, bike)?

   _____

   _____

5. How much will the materials cost?

   _____

   _____

6. What would you charge for this item or service?

   _____

   _____

7. What is your desired outcome for the business?

   _____

   _____

---

purpose of the learntrepreneur exercise is to expose your children to the elements of creativity, planning, implementation, success, and task completion. Each experience will benefit your children to some degree later in life.

Chapter Challenge ....

If you have earners over the age of twelve, ask them if they would like to try their own business. With the right amount of encouragement, they'll probably decide to give it a whirl. If so, help them pick out an idea for their learntrepreneur project. Sit down and help them write out a mini-business plan to answer the questions listed in this chapter. Be sensitive to their needs for independence, and offer only the help they need. Give them an opportunity to experience every challenge and reward. As they close in on their projected return on investment, encourage them and praise them for their accomplishments. Record the success in your family journal, and have your learntrepreneurs record their feelings about the experience.

....

CHAPTER 29

Keeping a Weekly Record

Setting a goal is not the main thing. It is deciding how you will go about achieving it and staying with that plan.

—Tom Landry

When Cash University was founded in 1996, it was based on a system that helped parents teach their children basic money management skills in the home. Up until that point, parents had few resources available for teaching their children these important skills. The Cash University money management system was developed because of this need.

The program contained many of the elements I have discussed thus far. Goal setting, earning, personal responsibility, and saving were among the skill areas reinforced by the system. The objective was to produce a program that would help parents work with their children to create a meaningful and lasting benefit. We wanted to produce something that a parent could use to teach financial lessons but also life skills and family communication. As you've probably discovered through the chapter challenges, communication levels go way up when you discuss ways to earn and what the family behavioral expectations may be. This communication by-product is a key benefit to your family as you learn to earn together.

The phrase Learn to Earn! has been the rallying cry for Cash University users. The earnings element is the most significant difference between the Cash University system and other family-based financial systems and books that are available. Helping children to understand where money comes from is perhaps the most important and overlooked element in their financial education today.

Most financial education resources focus on "the allowance" as a primary source of income for children. The adult counterpart to "the allowance" is a place in a government line no one would ever plan to frequent. Alternatively, most adults have some sort of occupation where they earn a living by providing a meaningful good or service to someone else. The children's counterpart to this earnings experience is what you are reading about right now. We as parents have the opportunity and responsibility to prepare our children to make a meaningful contribution. We can begin this preparation by helping them understand the value of concentrated effort toward an objective.

I've already discussed ways in which this can be done by assigning various tasks and negotiating a reasonable compensation for a job well done. I've also discussed household rules and expectations and the importance of predefining their consequences for children. A key factor in implementing these two strategies together is the creation of a weekly chart that tracks both jobs and responsibilities. With this chart, you can help your children get a visual "snapshot" of their weekly progress at any time. This chart will be a valuable tool for both you and your children as you monitor their weekly progress toward goal attainment. Visual aids enable us to physically mark accomplishments and consequences as they happen. This daily updating will create a tangible event for children. By providing real-time cause-and-effect documentation, you will create a deeply embedded learning experience for your children. We've included a sample of such a chart in Figure 29-2 on page 133. You may also visit KPM.com and print out Form TAC-1.

One of the most beneficial and rewarding "snapshots" to maintain for children is that of their goal item. By placing a picture of their goal item where they see it regularly, you can be assured that their motivation level to earn will stay high. By posting a picture on the bedroom wall or a bathroom mirror, my wife and I are able to keep our kids excited about the process. If one of the first things they see when they get out of bed is their objective, they'll be motivated to act in a purposeful and driven manner throughout the day.

This is true for any age group, including adults. How many times have you walked into the office of someone that is driven and discovered an inconspicuous photo or other motivating image placed somewhere in the office? I keep a photo of Ron Davis, former president and CEO of The Perrier Group of America, in my office. He's standing proudly next to this King Air, and the caption below states how he built his business, sold it, and now runs Davis Capital, LLC. "As a private pilot, Ron logs as many hours in his King Air as his busy schedule allows." For me, that's motivation to press on, work hard, and overcome all obstacles.

Goals play an important role in the development of self-motivation and personal drive. If we can help our children understand this and develop the habit of setting goals for themselves, we will make a substantial contribution to their ability to focus and achieve later in life. Figure 29-1 is an example of our goal reminder sheet. You can find this on KPM.com as Form GRS-1.

As you help your children visualize their goals, you must remember the three elements of effective goal attainment. By understanding these basic components, you can not only help your children attain their goals, but you'll be better able to set and attain goals for yourself.

The first of these elements is having a clearly defined and measurable objective. The more definite you can be on what your goal is, the more likely you are to attain it. Just as with many of the great athletes, visualize yourself crossing the finish line and meeting

Figure 29-1

GOAL REMINDER SHEET

Today's Date: _____

Name: _____

My Goal Is: _____

Dollars Needed: _____

Dollars Saved: _____

I Want to Reach My Goal by: _____

Start |--------|--------|--------|--------|--------| **Goal**
      20%   40%   60%   80%   100%   **Attained**

*Obstacles are those fearful things you see when you take
your eyes off your goal.*

—Henry Ford

---

your objective. In the case of your children, a picture with a price
tag will do nicely.

Once you're clear on your objective, set a time frame in which
you are determined to attain the goal. By giving yourself a deadline, your ability to stay motivated will remain high, your determination to attain the goal will increase as you near your deadline,
and your excitement about goal attainment will rise as you near
your objective. Procrastination will all but disappear as you
recognize the attainability of your goal within a predetermined
period of time.

After you've clearly visualized your objective with a tangible
value and given yourself a deadline for its attainment, you then

need to plan a detailed goal attainment process. As discussed earlier, this process is the action behind the attitude.

I've known many great goal *setters* in my business. They'll go to great lengths to set objectives, read the right motivational books, post their goal reminder cards, affirm how much they desire their objective, but then fail to take action. It's the effort, the work, the sweat—the GAP—that produces results. If you study the great achievers of the world, they all have one thing in common: the ability to take action. Planning without action is like building a high-performance race car that you never intend to drive. It's only the track time that counts.

To help your young savers become motivated and take action, you may want to provide some information to go along with their posted goal picture. This information would include how much the goal item costs and how long they think it will take to attain the goal. Once they've had the chance to think about these issues, have them write down their price and time-frame information to go along with their picture. This statement may read something like, "I will buy my new Roller Blades from Jim Shorts Sports for $55.00 by April 25." Have them place this statement near the goal picture, and have them read the statement aloud once in the morning and once at night before going to bed. By verbalizing their goal objective, they will begin to tap into a personal power that will propel them toward goal attainment.

If you have set some personal goals and objectives, you may want to try this idea for yourself. One of the first objectives I set for myself was to pay off a certain credit card balance by a certain date. I placed three-by-five note cards all over the place with my personal goal written on it. I had these cards in my car, in my bathroom, at my office, and in my bedroom. Everywhere I looked there was a goal attainment message motivating me to make the right decisions toward goal attainment.

As silly as it sounds, these three-by-five cards helped me focus on the objective and pay off the credit card debt within the time frame I had set for myself. If you've got a personal objective that you would like to attain, try writing yourself some goal reminder cards and putting them around your home and office. Read your cards out loud twice daily, and focus on the *action* necessary to accomplish your objective.

A written record of your objectives is important, but it's the *effort* that makes things happen. I've spent some time documenting what objectives are; now it's time to discuss how to get there and how to keep track of the goal attainment process. Effort is the key to any goal attainment, and keeping record of the daily events that constitute the goal attainment process is key. Some tools will help your children with this.

Figure 29-2 is an example of the Allowance Calculator. The weekly chart is broken down into two separate areas, "How to Make Money" and "How to Lose Money." Each area provides a place for documenting what goes on during the week.

"How to make Money" is where you can list the various opportunity jobs and their related payment amounts. Depending on the age and experience of your children, you may list many or only a few opportunities. Post this list in a prominent location; your children will see it regularly and become motivated to take action toward their goal attainment.

Likewise, "How to Lose Money" will be a reminder of the household rules and responsibilities. This is kind of like having speed limit signs posted along the highway. We are made aware of the changing speeds while driving because we are regularly reminded by a posted limit. Your children will be able to navigate the home environment easily by having limits and expectations clearly posted.

By posting a weekly chart of opportunities and responsibilities, you provide both the incentive for action as well as a vehicle to act. As a parent and teacher to your children, you'll find that a goal reminder sheet and an allowance calculator will be invaluable visual tools. They will work in tandem to help organize and direct

FIGURE 29-2

THE ALLOWANCE CALCULATOR

Name

Goal

Jobs

How to Make	+ $

S	M	T	W	T	F	S

Rules

How to Lose	– $

Payday ⟶ $ ☐

your children's efforts. Your children will learn and benefit from your orderly approach to helping them attain the objectives they have set for themselves. Together, the visual aids you create will promote a new family focus and clarity. As your children set goals and learn to earn, they will gain the life skills they need to design a life for themselves.

Chapter Challenge ....

Using the Goal Reminder Sheet and Allowance Calculator examples, design your own visual aids to use in working with your children. Make sure to include the price and attainment date on your goal sheet, and fill in the current opportunity jobs and responsibilities that have been agreed to within your family. If you have a personal objective that you would like to accomplish, you may want to try writing several positive goal affirmation cards for yourself. Place these cards in a number of different locations where you can see them and they will be a constant reminder to you of your dedication and commitment to reach the objective you have set for yourself. Write about the experience in your family journal. Have your children add a few comments about the process as well. For your convenience, the Allowance Calculator and Goal Reminder Sheet are available at KPM.com. You'll want to print out Forms TAC-1 and GRS-1 for each of your children.

BE AWARE OF YOUR EMOTIONS

CHAPTER 30

Predefined Consequences

*Once you have experienced excellence, you will never again
be content with mediocrity.*

—Thomas S. Monson

FAMILY RULES AND RESPONSIBILITIES ARE A LOT LIKE TRAFFIC LAWS
and road signs. When we drive, we are protected by the fact that
everyone around us knows, and mostly follows, the various traffic
laws and road signs. We can calmly and safely travel to our various
destinations without fear of harm or risk of injury. If another
driver decides to break the law and jeopardize our safety, public
servants on guard protect and serve us. Without these laws, posted
signs, and public servants, travel would be dangerous, nerve
wracking, and expensive. In a family, the parent acts as the public
servant. It is our job to police the little travelers who may or may
not decide to obey the posted family limits and laws. It's also our
job to make sure that the laws are understood and that the traffic
signs are clearly marked and unobstructed. We can't expect our little travelers to drive about safely if they don't understand the laws
and signs.

The family communication process is like a system of roads for
the flow of information. We have different kinds of roads for different kinds of travel. Big roads carry big issues at a fast pace.

Smaller secondary roads carry less significant bits of information at a slower pace along their scenic windings. Each system must be established to ensure that traffic doesn't get backed up and that the flow of information is unrestricted. At times there will be bottlenecks and repair work that needs to be done, but the overall quality of the drive depends on the individual drivers and the information they carry.

Major issues such as interpersonal relationships, family activities, and respect for others will be carried on the superhighways of our system. These roads must be clearly posted and well maintained. If these basic building blocks to our communications infrastructure are not well maintained, massive bottlenecks and long delays can be expected. If this is the case, the drive will be a tiresome one and the emotional strain of the trip will be great. If, on the other hand, we have built a solid six-lane superhighway and have made sure that the road is in good shape, we will be in for a most enjoyable and liberating experience. Just imagine what it's like on a bright sunny Saturday morning, by yourself on an open six-lane highway, headed for your favorite destination. After you implement a few of the suggested family communication ideas, this should be the new model of information flow within your home.

The secondary roads represent the enjoyable conversations we have with our spouses and kids. Talks about the day, vacation plans, and bedtime stories occupy these two-lane thoroughfares. If you picture a winding road through a New England countryside on a sunny fall morning, you may get a sense of how these communications can make you feel.

To get to these roads, however, you've got to head down the interstate for a few miles first. The quality of your secondary road experience will depend on how peacefully and safely you made it along the main thoroughfare. Make sure your main communication issues are well maintained and free of obstruction. Don't let these main arteries get clogged with broken-down issues because of a road that wasn't properly taken care of. If you keep all the lanes open, your information flow will be smooth and your secondary road travels will be an enjoyable experience for all family travelers.

Probably the best way to make sure your systems are free and clear is to ensure that your drivers know how to navigate. It's important for the safety of all who travel along these roads to make sure that all drivers have been made aware of the rules of the road. There's nothing more irritating than a foreign driver, unfamiliar with the process, driving 45 in the far-left lane.

Give your travelers the chance to understand the rules and expectations of driving the family communication highway. Let them know about the posted limits and what the consequences may be. Clearly define your role as public servant and emphasize that the laws will be enforced. Explain that all drivers will be treated equally and that when you drive on the family roads, you can feel safe and secure that your journey will be a positive and uplifting experience.

The vehicles we choose to drive are the individual conversation topics we introduce and how well we articulate those thoughts. We've got to be sure to think about what we want to say first. If you're not careful, there are some ridiculous things that can come out of your mouth. We can take the time to carefully assemble a vehicle that will last a lifetime, or we can throw together a machine that barely runs and is in need of repair often. We have the opportunity to create messages that are new and exciting that all family members want to experience. An example of such a message might be preparing the annual family vacation. One of the best ways we can maintain our vehicles is through participating in a family evening once a week.

We may sometimes, with good intentions, introduce something that just doesn't run that well, such as the year my family scheduled a Death Valley bike trip in August. The communication vehicle we ride in is made up of everything we stand for. We must carefully consider each vehicle in our garage before we put it on the road. Give it a good inspection, and make sure it drives well and that the mere appearance of the vehicle doesn't repulse other drivers. Just like when we are driving somewhere, we've got to be considerate of the other drivers on the road, give them plenty of space, and follow all rules.

The road conditions we face will be constantly changing. We'll all hit the occasional pothole, and we'll all get caught speeding once in a while. The way in which we react to these events will exemplify our character. We must strive to help our young family members experience a safe driving environment while they are in our county, because eventually they're going to get on the superhighway and keep going to other roads and other lands. Before they are faced with these new challenges, we need to make sure that they are great drivers and that they are capable of dealing with new and exciting real-life challenges.

One of the very first issues discussed in this book was the importance of defining the household rules. This is our first duty as traffic cop, to let the drivers know the laws. In order to prepare the transportation system for ease of access, it is important to define very clearly the expectations we parents have for our family members. A common mistake in many families is that they fail to define household rules and responsibilities. By allowing these issues to remain undefined, families leave themselves open to misunderstandings and miscommunication. If we, as family travelers, work together to establish a free flow of information, we eliminate many potential communication hazards in the future. This free flow of information is central to an environment that is free of emotional potholes and unexpected delays.

Chapter Challenge ....

The next time you and your family go for a drive, have your children identify the signs that represent rules of the road. Ask them what the signs mean and ask why they think the signs are there. Ask what benefit there might be to a particular posted rule. After several signs are discussed, ask your children what some of the signs in your house might read if the household rules were posted like the road signs. Ask why these household rules are important, and talk about the benefit of having some of the rules posted on the allowance calculator. You may want to write down any interesting comments from your younger travelers in your family journal.

....

CHAPTER 31

Family Emotions

You'll never give very good advice when you're mad.
—WILLARD S. STAWSKI II

IN MANY CASES, THE DIFFERENCE BETWEEN GOOD AND BAD parenting lies in emotions. If you allow yourself to get carried away in the moment and discipline your child out of emotion, you may need to rethink your process. I'm not saying that you shouldn't discipline your child, I'm saying that there is a right time and a right place for this activity. The right time is after you've had a chance to cool down and the right place is away from curious siblings that may be interested in watching the event.

To illustrate this point, consider the last time you were in the grocery store and saw a mother and her child struggling with "I want, I want, I want." How did the parent handle it, and to what degree did she allow her emotions to dictate her actions? The lower the degree of emotion, the higher the degree of effective parenting.

Children learn their behaviors through experience. If a child discovers that they can yell and scream and get their way, they'll perfect this technique. If the child is shown that yelling and screaming is ineffective, they'll abandon this tactic for the one that works better. It is only when the parent allows the child to receive positive reinforcement to bad behavior that the shopping scene will repeatedly manifest itself. This shopping scene is where parents are regularly emotionally tested.

A good example of rules, consequences, and emotion is the highway patrolman. You chose to drive 75 in a 65 mph zone, your radar detector went full scale to the red, and now you're sitting there with the patrol car behind you and all your friends passing you on the way to work. How you feel at that moment is how your kids feel when they get caught doing something wrong. How much worse would you feel if the officer decided to yell and scream at you about how dangerous it is to drive so fast and endanger the lives of the other drivers? How much worse do your kids feel when you yell and scream about how they need to take their shoes off before they come in from outside? How effective are the emotional outbursts?

If you were pulled over and were issued a ticket, did the officer decide what your penalty was going to be? Did he or she have the option to make up an amount on the spot, or were there posted amounts already in place to cover a variety of offenses? We all know the answers to these questions, and we all understand why the consequences must be predetermined. In society, law and order is based on fairness and justice. No one is deserving of any better treatment than anyone else for any reason. Likewise, in our homes, we need to be aware of the consequences of our rules, and we need to be fair in their administration. Nothing will cause your children to lose respect for you more quickly than if you impose an unfair consequence based on an emotional decision.

One of the biggest challenges we face as parents is how to be fair and objective when our children are intentionally trying to irritate us. We all know that children sit at home and plot ways in which they can get us upset. My philosophy is that kids, from when they are very young, are smarter than we are. They understand how we work and get a certain degree of enjoyment out of seeing us at our worst emotional whirlwind moments.

To counter this effect, we must be on guard. We can't let these little geniuses get the better of us. The most effective tool we have in our arsenal is the ability to figure out as much stuff that could go wrong as we can and predetermine our responses to such occasions. If we have decided beforehand what our response will be, we are effecting a counteraction, not a reaction. As the epigram to this chapter says, you'll never give good advice when you're mad. If we know ahead of time how we are going to respond to various family situations, we can avoid the embarrassing moments that so entertain our genius offspring.

Not all kids are all bad all the time. In a family, each child usually has one or two primary parental harassment techniques (PHTs) that he or she uses to get your attention. These tools will change over time as children grow and learn more sophisticated methods of harassment, but usually they'll limit their PHTs to only one or two at any given time. These PHTs represent the highest degree of impact your child will have on you and they know it. If your children aren't being given enough attention during the day, they typically will use a PHT to compensate. If you don't respond appropriately to them when they bring you a new discovery, a PHT may be just as effective.

Kids need attention no matter what, and they'll take negative attention over no attention any day. Remember, your kids are attention sponges, and you've got to help them feel important and understood. Without this understanding and positive attention, children will use plenty of PHTs, for the negative attention.

If we understand our children's inherent need for understanding and attention, we can avoid many of the negative behaviors that may develop in the home. When our children exhibit a PHT or two, we will want to diffuse the situation quickly using a predefined process. We can do this by posting the household rules and, if necessary, identifying the PHTs and their consequences. Our goal is to diffuse any potential situation before it's in our face.

Once we are aware of the attention needs of our children, we should provide them with an opportunity to receive the attention and understanding they demand. An excellent way for this to happen would be through a dedicated family night, set aside for fun and uplifting activities in the home. We'll discuss this fun and entertaining communication opportunity in greater detail in the next chapter.

Chapter Challenge ....

Identify the genius in your children. Observe how they interact with you and try to understand their attention needs. Watch what happens when you show them a high degree of attention, and compare it to their response when you may have not been so considerate. Identify your children's PHTs and discuss them openly. Record any thoughts in your family journal. Continue to use the Allowance Calculator and Goal Reminder Sheet and strive to limit the amount of negative emotion in your home.

....

....

CHAPTER 32

Family Night

If we die tomorrow, the company that we are
working for could easily replace us in a matter
of days, but the family we left behind will feel the
loss for the rest of their lives.

—ANONYMOUS

IT IS IMPORTANT FOR US TO UNDERSTAND THE COMMUNICATION
and attention needs of our children. You are the primary source of
information for them, and they will look to you as an example on
which to base many of their future decisions. To them, parents are
all-knowing and all-wise (at least until they turn thirteen). The
communication links you establish with your children are the
most important bonds you will ever create.

Take a moment to consider your communication levels with
each of your children. Think about some of the recent topics of
discussion that have come up and how deep you've gone into conversation about those topics. Did you listen to what they said, and
did your actions express a true interest in their concerns? It's
important for your children to be confident in both verbal and
nonverbal responses. They need to feel that they are as important
as anything else that may be on your mind.

Do you give your children the same consideration as you do your business and social associates, or do you simply pacify them with short polite responses? Many parents sometimes take the communication process with children for granted, especially when "life" gets busy. It's easy to get caught up in the daily grind and miss out on what your four-year-old has to tell you. Even though you don't have much energy left at the end of a long day, your junior communicator wants to ask, share, and express as soon as you walk in the door.

Most families probably maintain a pretty tight schedule and have each day and week committed far ahead. Good managers, in both business and domestic capacities, will make sure they make optimal use of their time every day. Scheduling is critical, and every commitment must be recorded. We've got business meetings, soccer practice, the PTA, Cub Scouts, Brownies, gymnastics, parent-teacher conferences, and on and on and on. Now let me ask a question. What goes on the schedule for the family? Not just Mom and the kids or Mom and Dad on a date (this one is really important, by the way), but where the whole family sits down together for a few hours to do something.

Now, the family vacation doesn't count, but it's a good start as long as it's not a long hot drive where everybody gets irritable. I'm talking about a regular time where everybody can sit down to talk about what's going on in the family. This is a time to reflect on the past week's activities and plan the next week.

If you're in business, regular department meetings need to happen. If you're at home, you may be active in a social or school group that meets regularly to conduct scheduled activities. Every organized entity on Earth, whether business, sport, social, or religious, conducts some sort of regular management or administrative meeting. These meetings usually happen on a predetermined date at a regularly scheduled time.

The results of these meetings are usually productive and promote a natural growth and development within the organization.

Concerns are addressed, conflicts resolved, and team unity strengthened. Management becomes more effective in their administration, and subordinates are motivated to be more productive and often become clearer on their necessity within the entity. The scheduled administrative meeting becomes central to the organized evolution and strength of the entity. The more frequent the meetings, the greater the growth and development within the organization. For example, a basketball team that practices daily is going to be significantly more effective than a team that practices weekly. A PTA group will accomplish more by meeting monthly than by meeting quarterly.

When we consider our family as a structured organization, how regularly scheduled meetings enhance the effectiveness of an organization and the communication needs of our children, we begin to understand how a family meeting night would be helpful. Conducting a weekly family meeting will reinforce elements of stability, togetherness, communication, and direction.

If we have a regularly scheduled block of time each week for family time, our children will gain a degree of stability in their lives. They will look forward to this time as a way to reinforce relationships and feel safe, secure, and stable in a world that is not.

By meeting weekly as a family, relationships are enhanced and the family unit is more clearly defined. In this day and age of tremendously challenging outside influences, togetherness as a family becomes more important. Children need to feel that they belong first and foremost to a family and secondarily to a social group away from the home. This order is being reversed more and more often as parents take less responsibility in their homes.

By conducting a family evening, communication among family members will be enhanced and the barriers that sometimes exist will come down. The most important skill you can develop as a parent is the ability to talk to your child. This is a critical point, and you need to comprehend its significance.

THE MOST IMPORTANT SKILL YOU CAN DEVELOP AS A PARENT

IS THE ABILITY TO TALK TO YOUR CHILD.

The media are beginning to focus on the importance of family communication skills, perhaps because of recent violent outbursts in schools. Youth contributors to a CNN Town Meeting on April 29, 1999, strongly emphasized the need for "our parents to talk with us." Children need to be able to talk, learn, and ask questions. This communication need is central to children's growth and development. They are born empty slates and learn everything through communication. They will always be learning, wherever they are, whether it's at school, with friends, or at home. Home is the best place to learn most things, and a weekly family evening will provide a time and a location for an excellent learning opportunity.

A weekly family evening will help you define your family's direction as well. Where is your family going, and what are your family objectives? Do you have a family goal? If so, what is your charted course to get to that goal? This common objective will help family members feel as if they are working together toward something. Our kids need to feel as if they are part of the journey, as if they can contribute meaningfully to the family cause. We can help our children develop this sense of contribution by having defined family objectives, supported by a family evening.

By creating the habit of a weekly family meeting night, each family member will grow in strength, self-esteem, family appreciation, and family commitment. Family stability will be enhanced, family members will desire to be together, communication levels will increase significantly, and a common family goal will define the family direction. The home should be our children's safe haven from the outside world. The weekly family evening will provide the opportunity for that safe haven to develop.

Chapter Challenge ....

Pick out one night of the week that is most easily reserved
for a regular family activity (ours is Monday night) and set
it aside for your family night. Sit down now as a family and
discuss the importance of this time together. Ask your children what they would like to do as a fun activity during this
time. Write the results in your family journal. Read the next
chapter before your first meeting.

....

....

CHAPTER 33

Family Night Outline and Ideas

You can discover more about a person in an hour of play than in a year of conversation.

—PLATO

IN CHAPTER 32 WE TALKED ABOUT THE BENEFITS OF HAVING A weekly time set aside for a family night. In this chapter we'll discuss some ideas that will make your family night a time that is productive for family members, full of fun, and looked forward to by everyone.

One of the greatest advantages to the family night is that it will provide an opportunity for everyone to review their progress toward their personal goals. As we've worked together through this book, you've been writing down some personal goals, setting aside some opportunities to earn, defining the household responsibilities, and communicating at a higher level because of these activities. The family night will provide a regular time in which we can evaluate our progress, discuss the jobs that are being done, offer new opportunities, discuss responsibilities, and keep everyone excited about how great it is being in the same family.

We've laid the groundwork for an orderly and structured learning environment for our children. We want our children to grow up and be effective young adults, prepared for the real world. The steps outlined in this book will help you accomplish your objectives. The family night will give you a weekly opportunity to make sure you're still on track with your family's development. Through the family night, each and every family member will more clearly understand the family's big picture and the role that they play in that picture.

The purpose of the family night isn't to drill your kids into the ground and make them little production robots but to reinforce the family togetherness environment and to make sure that all family members are progressing to the best of their ability toward the objectives that they have set for themselves. Your role as family leader is to make sure that the family night is fun, rewarding, and eagerly anticipated. You can do this by having a plan that outlines various ideas and activities that your family can do together during this time. An example of such a plan is shown in Figure 33-1 and can also be found on KPM.com as Form FNP-1.

A typical family night might be:

6:00–6:30 P.M.: Have dinner. (Save dessert for later.)

6:30–6:45 P.M.: Clean up dining area and kitchen together.

6:45–7:00 P.M.: Prepare the activities. Kids can gather their goal sheets and earnings calculators for review.

7:00–7:45 P.M.: Read the family motto and family mission statement aloud. Discuss any issues or concerns that are ongoing from the previous week or new. Discuss the family night activity and lesson: Review earnings calculators, goal sheets, any spending, family goal, and family journal.

7:45–8:00 P.M.:   All family members get to say one thing that bothered them over the last week and two things that made them happy.

8:00–8:15 P.M.:   Dessert time.

8:15–9:00 P.M.:   Family night activity and lesson.

The last event in your family night is the family activity and lesson. This may be structured around a specific family need or something that is currently in the media. You may choose to use this time to read together or discuss current events. Don't be too concerned or intimidated by the need to be creative with your family; everyone will be happy with whatever you choose to do.

You can develop a number of unique and family-specific activities that will benefit each member of your family. No one knows your family better than you do, and once you choose a topic, you'll be surprised at your ability to design fun and challenging lessons and activities yourself. You may even want to have your children participate in the activity design. By working together to create your family activities and lessons, you'll enhance the experience for all involved.

Below you will find a list of forty family-based lesson ideas for your consideration:

1. Why we have adversity in our lives
2. How we can grow from our challenges
3. Respecting our leaders: family, school, government
4. Household rules and laws: Why are they necessary?
5. Loving our country, history, Constitution
6. How to be a good citizen
7. How to settle conflict fairly
8. Our judicial system
9. Counting our blessings

FIGURE 33-1

FAMILY NIGHT PLANNING SHEET

For the Night of _____

Location _____

Tonight's Theme Is _____

DINNER (Everybody pitch in) _____

    Cook _____

    Set Table _____

    Serve _____

    Clear Table _____

    Dishes _____

ACTIVITY PREPARATION

    Materials Needed _____

    _____

    Gather Weekly Charts _____

TEAM TIME

    Family Motto _____

    Read Family Mission Statement _____

    Family Issues _____

    Family Concerns _____

    Review: Kids' Earning, Spending, Goals, and Progress

        Notes: _____

        _____

FIGURE 33-1   *(Continued)*

Review: Family Goal, Progress, Issues, Family Journal

Notes: _____

_____

Review: What bugged you last week? (anybody)

Notes: _____

_____

What did you do to fix it? _____

_____

Review: What was great about last week? (everybody)

Notes: _____

_____

DESSERT TIME

Prepare _____

Serve _____

Cleanup _____

ACTIVITY AND LESSON

Topic _____

Instructing _____

Notes: _____

CLOSING

Next Week's Theme _____

Materials Needed _____

Setup _____

10. Why it's important to be dependable

11. Keeping the promises we make to others

12. Why we shouldn't hold grudges

13. How to be a true friend to others

14. How to make and keep friends

15. Maintaining personal standards

16. Our family tree; knowing our ancestors

17. Looking for the good in others

18. Being thankful for what you have

19. The importance of being honest

20. The importance of being humble

21. Keeping the family journal.

22. The family motto

23. The family mission statement

24. Learning to enjoy learning

25. Learning to earn

26. Learning to listen to others

27. Social etiquette, good manners

28. Keeping a financial record

29. The personal net worth statement

30. The importance of finding the right spouse

31. Intelligent dating

32. Controlling the media in our homes

33. Recognizing quality in what we buy

34. Learning to set priorities

35. The importance of speaking well

36. Communication skills, listen more than you talk

37. Why self-control is important

38. How to be self-reliant

39. The importance of a quality effort in all you do

40. Life planning

From these suggestions, you should be able to put together quite a few fun and informative family activities and lessons. By planning ahead, the family member responsible for lesson preparation (usually a parent or older child) will find a great deal of personal satisfaction as a result of their efforts. Other resources for lesson preparation can be found online by searching key words, through local libraries, or at your local church or synagogue.

The enhanced family skills that will develop from a regularly scheduled family night will make a significant impact on each member of your family that will last a lifetime. This weekly forum will help educate family members as well as unite them toward a common goal. Remember, *no material success you can attain will ever make up for a failure in the home.* The family night will provide you with the balance you need to offset your otherwise demanding schedule away from home.

Chapter Challenge ....

Pick a lesson idea from the list that best relates to the fun activity selected during the last chapter challenge. Combine the lesson idea with your fun activity to organize your first family night. As a guideline, follow the outline provided in this chapter, modifying it as you see fit. Form FNP-1 from KPM.com may also be helpful. Have a great time. Record any significant developments in your family journal.

....

SAVING AND PERSONAL RECORD KEEPING

Up to this point I've discussed a number of key family and financial topics. I began by discussing the formation of your family team and promoted that team by creating a family motto, family mission statement, and family journal. Once all family members understood that they were working together toward a common objective, I then touched on helping children understand the household rules and their family responsibilities. As children began to understand the importance of their participation, I talked about family jobs, opportunity jobs, and how to earn. The importance of goal setting was emphasized, and the process of mapping out a path to goal attainment was covered. I then discussed the difference between a job and a career and the basics of life planning.

Everything I've discussed thus far is pertinent to attaining the necessary life skills to be financially and family literate. The foundation that has been prepared is solid and ready to be built upon. The following section, about personal record keeping, draws on many of the areas previously covered. Now I will take the skills developed over the last several sections and apply them to real-life issues for the benefit of you and your children.

CHAPTER 34

Your Family Budget

This is not a dress rehearsal. This is it.

—TOM CUNNINGHAM

ONE OF THE GREATEST THINGS WE AS PARENTS CAN DO TO INCREASE the peace and happiness in our homes and to set a good example for our children is to make sure that our personal finances are in order. In this day and age when one in two marriages ends in divorce, financial difficulties are listed as the number-one cause of stress in the home. This stress leads to other problems and then to eventual marital demise. Once we understand the consequences of financial mismanagement, we can protect ourselves from its effect through a little bit of thinking and a little bit more of a thing called discipline.

A two-word phrase accurately summarizes the cause for the difference between financial peace and financial stress. This phrase accounts for the difference between a family that has the financial resources to do what it wants when it wants and a family that lives from moment to moment, hoping that something happens to change its miserable financial state. No one can look upon this phrase with indifference. People regard it with either negative or positive emotion, depending on their financial state.

Those with financial peace love the phrase and appreciate its

meaning to the fullest extent. Most older citizens grew up understanding the significance of these words and still live by them
today. Also, most financial professionals understand the benefit of
the phrase and promote it to their clients as often as possible.

Those with financial stress most likely look upon the phrase as
an unpopular idea whose time has come and gone, an idea that
limits rather than liberates, one that is unnecessary during a time
of such prosperity and abundance. If they only knew how to
implement the phrase, it actually would liberate them from their
financial bonds.

The two words that I refer to are *gratification deferral.* Those
who are able to save and invest have mastered the habit of gratification deferral. Those who must have everything they want right
now do so at the sacrifice of the future.

In the media today, everything is aimed at getting what you
want right now, when you want it. If you think about the recent
popularity of the automobile lease, you'll understand what is
happening. Never before has such a large depreciating asset been
made available for so little every month over such extended
terms. Never before has so much debt been made available for the
equity in a home. People are now financing their vehicles for up
to seventy-two months and longer and are taking home equity
loans for up to 125% of the value of their homes.

Statistically, we can now see both the cause and effect of
financial illiteracy. Earlier I discussed the massive consumer debt
and record levels of bankruptcy; that's the effect. The cause is
seventy-two-month car contracts and 125% home equity loans.
The only way to break the cycle is to recognize the problem,
make a commitment to do something about it, and then really
do something about it. That's what personal budgeting is all
about.

So, what's the first step in releasing your financial bonds and
gaining your financial freedom? It's not to call toll-free with your
credit card and send me $129.95 over three easy payments to get

your "I Want It All Right Now" miracle kit. Such instant success programs rarely work out for the purchaser.

The answer is not to regularly purchase lottery tickets either. You've got a better chance of being run over by a truck than you do winning the lottery. So if you can't purchase an effective get-rich-now kit anywhere, and you're not going to win the lottery, what can you do?

It's actually quite easy. First, cut up any nonessential credit cards with a balance of over $500. Come on, I know you've done it before. Why not do it again, but this time make it stick? The only cards I'll allow you to keep are the ones with a zero balances at the end of the month. If you pay off the cards you use and are able to maintain zero balances, then you're probably disciplined enough to hang on to them. Also, if you travel a lot you'll need to keep one active to purchase airline tickets, for car rentals, and for hotel expenses, but other than that, get rid of those high-interest freedom binders. Besides, for most purchases, if you don't have the cash, you probably don't need it. Not spending with credit cards is the core of gratification deferral. If you use your cards all the time, you are an instant gratification junkie and are most likely headed in the wrong direction.

Once you've eliminated the temptation in your wallet and stopped your financial bleeding, you need to get yourself healthy and on the road to financial recovery. You've got to identify whom you owe what and get everybody paid off as quickly as possible.

Now, if you're like me, I used to hate going to the mailbox. Each trip to the street was like rolling the dice to find out what's due today. At one point, my wife and I had over a dozen different credit cards. We would get a new bill *every other day.* How is a young family ever going to establish a healthy financial environment with that kind of pressure? We had a problem that we needed to fix, and we did it.

The first thing we did was put together a basic budget for ourselves. This was pretty easy because we knew how much our monthly expenses were and how much our income was. If you're not on a budget yet, you need to make one now. Once you're done cutting up your credit cards, sit down and list your income and expenses. Figure out how much you're spending every month on rent, utilities, groceries, transportation, and entertainment, and give yourself some limits to live within. We introduced a basic budget template back in chapter 4; now it's time to put it to work. Either follow the format shown there or go to KPM.com and print out Form BGT-1. Nothing else we do in this section will matter until you build your family budget, so do it now if you haven't already. Use the format shown in Figure 4-1 on pages 18–19.

The next thing we did was make a list of all our card and loan balances. From the gas card with a couple of hundred dollars on it to the lease on the BMW, we listed everything, from lowest and easiest to pay off, up to the most challenging nonhome debt. Back in chapter 2, we had you create a debt repayment schedule with a commitment to paying off your smallest debt within 60 days. Review your progress on that payoff and the debt list you created. Keep a copy of that debt list in a place where you will review it and update it regularly. You should plan to go to KPM.com and print out a new Form CC-2 about every ninety days to reevaluate your debt elimination progress.

Once you have a budget and know what you want to pay off, you can combine the two and begin your journey to financial freedom. This is serious business, and you need to be committed to eliminating your obligations. You must budget your dollars very carefully and have an exact amount left over every paycheck that can be allocated to debt reduction.

If you owe more each month than you earn, professional credit counseling centers are available to help you work out a plan with your creditors. If you are indeed upside down at the end of the month, you need to make a call immediately to get working on a plan. The Web site for the National Foundation for Consumer

Credit (www.nfcc.org) was designed to give consumers detailed information on the credit counseling centers across the country available to help with credit problems.

If you aren't upside down, you will use any dollars that are left over to pay on the smallest obligation outstanding. Once that obligation is gone, you need to begin to work on the next largest balance on your list. As your obligations are eliminated, the monthly amount available for debt reduction will become larger.

As we implemented this plan for ourselves, before we knew it, we had eliminated what we owed on our six lowest-balance credit cards and were getting bad news in the mail every three days instead of every other day. Shortly thereafter we eliminated three more debts completely, and our misery mail lessened to one piece every four days. Things were starting to happen, and financial peace was being restored to our family.

Once we got down to two revolving debts, we decided to establish an emergency fund for our family. We wanted to make sure that if anything happened to us, we would be covered for at least a month. Our monthly budget at the time was around $3,000, and we wanted to have those funds available in an account just in case. Knowing that you're covered for at least thirty days goes a long way toward enhancing the family's financial and emotional stability.

With two cards left and a decent budget surplus, we split the excess cash two ways. Half went toward the card elimination and half went toward the emergency fund. Before long, our thirty-day emergency fund was established and we were down to only one card left to pay off. At that point, we decided to continue building our emergency fund to sixty days and give ourselves that much extra breathing room. Within six months, all our credit cards were paid off and we had accumulated a two-month budget savings established. We had learned our lesson the hard way and pulled through together to establish a comforting degree of financial stability for our family.

Our next objective was to establish savings accounts for the kids and a retirement savings plan for ourselves, but we'll talk about that in chapter 37.

Chapter Challenge ....

Review your personal budget and debt elimination plans. Make sure that you have implemented both components and have shared the experience with your appropriately aged children. Discuss gratification deferral with your older children; explain what it means, and show them how it may apply to existing debts that you may have. Explain your debt reduction strategy to them. Keep accurate records and commit to a monthly budget and a proactive debt elimination plan.

....

CHAPTER 35

Your Children's Budget

Sometimes when learning comes before experience
it doesn't make sense right away.

—RICHARD BACH

CHAPTER 29 REVIEWED THE USES OF THE GOAL REMINDER SHEET and the allowance calculator. The goal reminder sheet gives us the ability to motivate our children through the formation of an objective that is attainable within a certain time period. The allowance calculator gives us the ability to track our children's earning and responsibility progress throughout the week. As we accumulate our children's allowance calculator pages over time, we should begin to notice a progression in their abilities and determination. Goal items should be getting larger, and efforts should become refined as children develop pride in the earnings process. As they experience what it's like to accomplish a task to the best of their abilities, their appreciation for self-direction will grow naturally and their self-esteem will increase appropriately.

If you've found that your children are utilizing the opportunities to set, work on, and meet objectives, you may choose to introduce a checkbook into your system. A checkbook will provide children with an excellent opportunity to keep track of where their money came from and where it went. In its most basic form, the checkbook provides children with their first experience in budgeting. As they grow to understand the basic workings of the checkbook, they prepare themselves for more sophisticated budgeting techniques later in life. Financial intelligence requires the mastery of basic elements before more sophisticated principles are understood.

By using a checkbook, your children will have access to their earnings at any given time. You can find a children's checkbook at virtually any teachers' or educational toy store. I've found them from as low as five dollars to as much as fifteen dollars. By adding a checkbook to your existing goal-setting and earning tools, you will complete the last component of a powerful learning system for your children. As an addition to your system, the checkbook will give your children the chance to budget their own earnings and will enable them to make purchase and value decisions. For the first time, your children will be able to make a real-world financial decision before they're out on their own. The more practice they can get while in the safety of their own home, the better equipped they will be to navigate a real-world financial environment.

The children's checkbook you purchase will work like any other checkbook an adult may carry. Use the allowance calculator to create deposits for the checkbook by tracking and accumulating the jobs that are done in exchange for compensation throughout the week. At the end of the week, usually on Friday, sit down with your children and calculate all earnings to create a "deposit" into the checkbook register. The checkbook then becomes a vehicle whereby children have access to their own earnings. When children carry their checkbook with them, they will have the chance to make value-based decisions concerning whether an item is worth the purchase price. Only when they've earned the money themselves does this issue take on significance.

When my wife and I first started the system by experimenting on our children, we discovered that the kids were much more likely to spend *our money* on useless junk than their own money. When it was *their* hard-earned cash at stake, they were much more apt to be frugal. Ordinarily they would have begged and pleaded for items that now they would put back. Once they had their own source of money, the kids began making their own buying decisions and we as parents were out of the impulse-toy-buying business. As our children gained experience in shopping with their own money, they began to develop their own sense of value and standards for quality. They began to understand why the cheapest item isn't always the better buy. They began to look for items that were on sale and to conserve their resources. The skills that they were learning by having their own earnings and checkbook early on were teaching them the gratification deferral skills that we as parents had missed when we grew up. Once they were used to having their own money available, they became more selective in their spending.

By now you've spent some time with your children working on the basics of goal setting, earning, and the goal attainment process. Most likely your children have learned a few new skills, including how to set an objective, take on family responsibilities, and work around the house to earn money toward their goal. I hope they've had the chance to attain one or two goal items and have experienced the pride of ownership that accompanies such an accomplishment. The introduction of a checkbook will be a natural progression for your children at this point. The checkbook will add a degree of pride and accomplishment and will round out the earning, saving, and spending cycle. By introducing them to the basic checkbook today, you'll prepare them to understand and appreciate more sophisticated budgeting principles tomorrow.

Chapter Challenge ....

Visit a local teachers' or educational toy store and locate a children's checkbook to use with your children. You can also order one at www.cashuniversity.com or at KPM.com. Show them how to write out a check and help them understand the checkbook register. Make a "deposit" into the register with any monies that have been earned, and give them a bonus amount for the new book. Take the children with you the next time you go shopping, and watch them as they pick out an item to buy. Have them write out a check to you for the amount of the item including tax (an even dollar amount is the easiest), and give them cash to make the purchase themselves. Help them record the transaction in their register, and make an entry in the family journal about the experience.

If you have children over the age of twelve, you'll want to go to KPM.com and check out the link to www.pocket card.com. This innovative debit card for kids can replace the checkbook and give your children a real-world experience in money managment.

....

CHAPTER 36

Gambling, Borrowing, and Saving

I hear and I forget. I see and I remember.
I do and I understand.

—Anonymous

THIS CHAPTER IS PROBABLY THE CLOSEST I'VE COME TO GOING over the moral or ethical edge. I wrote it from a purely educational standpoint and have included it to illustrate several important financial intelligence considerations.

Thus far the text has discussed a number of proactive steps to teach our children about setting goals, looking for opportunity, earning, saving, and using a checkbook. These basics, if reinforced regularly, will come to form the foundation of your children's financial intelligence. Ultimately, the skills they are learning today will provide them with a sound basis for a lifetime of quality, unemotional, and logical financial decision making.

Even though your children are gaining insight into the financial basics, there are still some hazards out there that they should be made aware of at an early age. Credit, debt, and the careless spending of resources are all topics we can review with our children early on. I discuss credit and debt later in this chapter, but first let's help our children understand the value of their earnings and how quickly those earnings can disappear in the wrong environment.

As adults, one of the risks we can take with our money is by betting or gambling. Even lately, with some of the dot-com companies fluctuating wildly in the market, these transactions seem more like gambling than investing. While this form of recreation may be fun and exciting, very few participants in these activities can consistently win and net a profit. For the rest of the gambling public, participating in these risk activities increases the potential for loss of financial control and eventual catastrophe. Just attend a Gamblers Anonymous meeting to get an earful of how lives have changed because of the gambling disease. As parents, we have the responsibility to our children to tell them about gambling and to help them understand the possibility of substantial net loss as a result of their participation.

We can accomplish this lesson by giving them a personal gambling experience. Now, I'm not suggesting that you haul your kids off to Vegas and turn them loose in a room full of slot machines. What I am suggesting is to illustrate to them the details of a crafty industry, designed to take away their hard-earned dollars with very little chance of return.

Most parents I know don't consider video arcades or carnivals to be a potential hazard to their children. Most don't think twice about letting their children attend these events regularly and freely provide them the cash necessary to participate in their games and activities. This participation, in moderation, is fine and represents very little long-term risk to children.

As parents, we want to protect our children from spending their money on foolish activities and wasting their resources. We also want to teach them positive financial lessons that will aid them throughout their lifetimes. Both of these experiences can happen in arcades or at carnivals where tickets can be won by playing games and then exchanged for prizes at a prize counter, depending on how the experience is presented. The lessons can be facilitated easily, they'll be fun for the kids, and you'll incur only a small financial expense.

The environment will provide families with an example of a certain level of pregambling conditioning and can enable children to be made aware of how quickly their hard-earned dollars can disappear.

If you carefully analyze what happens at these "kiddy casinos," you'll be surprised at the sophistication of the financial desensitization that takes place. Typically, on arrival at the arcade or carnival, currency must be exchanged, or "revalued," into an alternative spending medium, usually tokens or tickets. Once people have the tokens or tickets, they can participate in various games of chance or mild skill that may yield an additional form of currency, the "game ticket." These game tickets can be accumulated to purchase prizes from the prize counter at an inflated price. Children who are allowed to participate in these activities without parental supervision are rapidly desensitized to the value of their currency and are systematically prepared to enjoy other forms of games of chance as adults.

Such experiences may be harmful to children if they are left to themselves to deduce the effects of their activities. If, on the other hand, children have been made aware of the value of earning and saving and have grown to understand the value of the dollars they are about to lose, the experience can have a substantial and lifelong positive impact, especially if the parent participates in the learning process.

The next time you visit one of these locations, make sure your children have brought along their checkbook. On the way there, you may want to reiterate the things they had to do to obtain the dollars they are about to spend. Also talk about the fun that you're going to have, but keep them focused on observing where their money goes. You may even want to help them keep track of their expenses and winnings in a small notebook.

Once you arrive at the arcade or carnival, have your young adventurers write you a check for the money they plan to spend and then give them the cash. Help them exchange their money for tokens or tickets, and walk them through the games and activities they wish to participate in. Make sure you have an enjoyable time while you're out, but try to stay focused on the lessons of the visit.

As they spend their money, keep track of what they have done and any tickets they win. More than likely, the amount of money they have won't last very long and they'll be asking you for a little financial assistance. Once this happens, take your "little gamblers" aside and review the events that just transpired. Talk again about how hard it was to earn the dollars they just spent and review how much more quickly the money was spent than earned. Make sure they comprehend the results of the lesson and appreciate the difference between saving and spending.

Once they understand the value of this lesson, give them back their check and let them know that the lesson was on you. You may want to give them some spending money for the rest of your visit to show how cool a parent you really are. Really enjoy the time with your children and help them know how much you care about them. When you're done playing, on the way home, review the lessons learned again. Ask them what the most important thing they learned during the visit was, and make sure they comprehend the value of the experience.

Many young college students wind up in trouble because of their mismanagement of personal credit card resources. It was recently reported that three college students from different campuses committed suicide because of what were, to them, unmanageable credit card balances. In all cases, the balances were relatively low and would have been manageable if the student had any financial intelligence. Credit and debt management has become a serious issue that we must make sure our children are prepared to deal with.

An effective way to teach debt management is to give your children some practical experience by allowing them to borrow from you for an item that they would like to have. If your children are expressing a desire for something that they can't afford at the time, you may have an opportunity to conduct a financial lesson. Figure 36-1 is a standard borrowing contract that you can use to teach a simple lesson about borrowing and the responsibilities of having debt.

The form can be found on KPM.com as Form Note-1 for your convenience. The way this note will work for your family is very simple. Calculate the price of the item that the children would like to have. Make sure that the value is inexpensive enough that it can be repaid within several weeks of ordinary earning around the house. Review the note with your soon-to-be borrower and help them understand the commitment they are about to enter into. Make sure they have at least 20% of the value of what they want to buy as a down payment, and then supply the rest of the funds needed to purchase the item.

Calculate equal payments including an interest amount for the duration of the note. For example, if the item they wanted to buy costs $100, have them pay $20 down and finance the other $80 with your own money. Charge them interest of $10 for the right to borrow, and set the payoff balance at $90. (It is easier to work with round numbers.) Fill in the repayment schedule on the note for equal payments, and have them sign it before the purchase. Before they sign the note, let them know that whatever it is that they are buying will become the "collateral" for the right to borrow. Make sure that they understand that if they "default" on the loan, you'll be forced to "repossess" the "collateral," and the entire note will be due at once. By repossessing their collateral, you'll take away the item that was purchased with borrowed funds. If this happens, let your children feel the pressure of having the entire note due and assist them in finding extra work around the house to quickly earn back the difference. Do not allow them to walk away from their obligations; this could have devastating

FIGURE 36-1

FAMILY BORROWING CONTRACT

GENERAL

Date _____

Name of Borrower _____

Name of Lender _____

Item to Be Purchased _____

Location _____

Why I've Got to Have It Now _____

_____

PRICING

Retail Price of Item $_____

Any Sale or Purchase Discount   – $_____

Sale Price $_____

Sales Tax (_____%)   + $_____

Purchase Price $_____

FINANCING

Purchase Price $_____

Financing Charges (10%)   +$_____

Total Cost $_____

PAYMENT CONTRACT

Total Cost $_____

Down Payment (20%)   – $_____

Total Financed $_____

Number of Payments _____

Amount of Payment $_____

FIGURE 36-1 *(Continued)*

PAYMENT SCHEDULE

DATE	AMOUNT
_____	$ _____
_____	$ _____
_____	$ _____
_____	$ _____
_____	$ _____
_____	$ _____
_____	$ _____
_____	$ _____

Projected Payoff Date: _____

Late Charges: $_____

Borrower agrees to make payments on time and will take care of purchase item. Borrower agrees that if the payment is more than two days late, a late charge will be assessed. Borrower agrees that the item purchased will be used as collateral until the item is paid in full. Borrower agrees that if two or more payments are missed in this contract, lender may repossess the item purchased and all payments will be due immediately. Lender agrees to help borrower by providing good opportunities to earn money to pay off this loan. Lender further agrees to help borrower keep track of when payments are due and to explain all elements of this contract.

SIGNED

_____   _____
Borrower   Lender

_____   _____
Date   Date

OBJECTIVE SATISFIED

I HEREBY CERTIFY THAT THE DEBT ORIGINATED THROUGH THIS LOAN CONTRACT HAS BEEN SATISFIED IN FULL AND THAT THE BORROWER EXECUTED HIS/HER RESPONSIBILITY BY MAKING ALL PAYMENTS.

_____   _____
Lender   Date

consequences. If they are in agreement with these terms, fill in the appropriate blanks on the note and have the borrowers sign the document. As soon as you sign it, give the borrower the cash necessary for them to make their purchase. Once they have made their purchase, staple the receipt "title" to the note and let them know that they can have both back when the note is satisfied.

As the borrower earns throughout the week, remind them of the importance of making a timely weekly payment and help them understand that they will need to earn enough to have some spending money left over after the payment. Each Friday, ensure a full payment is made and that the deduction is made out of their earnings total in their checkbook register. Hold on to the checks as they are written and maintain a record of payment. Staple the "canceled" checks to their loan document.

Give your borrower the opportunity to pay the note off early if they want to. Encourage them to work a bit harder to earn as much extra as they can to pay down the debt. You may even rebate the interest fee if they can pay off the note within a certain period of time. Give them every possible opportunity to get out of debt.

Once the borrower has repaid their debt, let them know how proud you are of them and give them an opportunity to borrow again. It is hoped that the pressure caused by indebtedness made them determined not to go into debt again. If, however, they paid the note off without any undue personal hardship, they may want to try it again with a larger item. If they seem to be developing a sense of responsibility through the process, help them again and encourage the additional responsibility and personal commitment to repay.

This exercise does not aim to encourage children to become debtors; rather, it seeks to promote a degree of personal responsibility and commitment. As children begin to be more adept at managing their responsibilities, the parent may want to use a family savings agreement to help them develop a structured savings program toward a specific objective. The structured savings plan is a kind of reverse note or "lay-away" program. Instead of borrowing up front, the parent can record an initial deposit and then make a weekly deposit commitment toward a goal. Instead of being charged interest on the transaction, savers actually can be credited toward their efforts. Figure 36-2 is an example of a family savings agreement. This chart can be printed out from KPM.com by referring to Form FSA-1.

When implementing a family savings agreement, you'll want to make sure that the item being saved for is available when the children attain their goal. You'll also want to make sure that any discount on the price is retained early on in the contract. The best way to accomplish this is to actually purchase your children's agreed-to savings objective. By having the goal item in the home, you'll not only make sure that pricing and availability are set, but you'll also provide a substantial in-house incentive to meet the objective. If your young saver sees their objective, just sitting there waiting to be paid for, they'll be highly motivated to get busy and follow through with their agreement.

Just as in the borrowing example, make sure the saver has at least 20% to deposit toward their objective. Calculate a 10% bonus based on the total value of the goal item. Subtract this amount from the total due and figure a net amount due. For example, if your savers' goal costs $100, make sure they have at least $20 to start the account. Then add an amount of $10 as a saving interest incentive to the account; thus only $70 remains to attain the objective. Calculate between four to eight equal payments for the duration of the contract and have your saver commit to the process. Take a moment to review the difference between borrowing and saving with your children. Through the note, children would have to pay an extra $10 in interest to purchase an item. By savings through a family savings agreement, the children were was able to earn a $10 saving bonus. The difference between the two strategies is $20 net. These two forms should serve as ample

FIGURE 36-2

FAMILY SAVINGS AGREEMENT

GENERAL

Date _____

Name of Saver _____

Name of Lender _____

Item to Be Purchased _____

Location _____

Why I Can Wait to Get It _____

_____

PRICING

Retail Price of Item	$	_____
Any Sale or Purchase Discount	– $	_____
Sale Price	$	_____
Sales Tax (_____%)	+ $	_____
Purchase Price	$	_____

SAVING

Purchase Price	$	_____
Saving Bonus (10%)	– $	_____
Total Cost	$	_____

SAVINGS AGREEMENT

Total Cost	$	_____
Deposit	– $	_____
Total Needed	$	_____

Number of Deposits _____

Amount of Each Deposit $_____

Figure 36-2 *(Continued)*

DEPOSIT SCHEDULE

Date	Amount	Extra	Bonus
_____	$_____	_____	$_____
_____	$_____	_____	$_____
_____	$_____	_____	$_____
_____	$_____	_____	$_____
_____	$_____	_____	$_____
_____	$_____	_____	$_____
_____	$_____	_____	$_____
_____	$_____	_____	$_____

Projected Payoff Date: _____

Lender agrees to add a bonus of _____% each time an extra payment is deposited to the goal savings account. This bonus will reduce the Saver's over-all cost and will enable the Saver to reach the goal in a shorter period of time.

SIGNED

_____   _____
Saver   Lender

_____   _____
Date   Date

OBJECTIVE SATISFIED

I HEREBY CERTIFY THAT THE SAVER DID COMPLETE THE OBJECTIVE AND HAS ACCUMULATED ENOUGH CURRENCY TO PURCHASE THE GOAL ITEM. I FURTHER CERTIFY THAT THROUGH SAVINGS DILIGENCE, SAVER EARNED A DISCOUNT OF $_____ OFF THE GOAL ITEM PURCHASE PRICE.

_____
Lender

_____
Date

evidence that it is better to save than to borrow. This lesson will illustrate the importance and benefit of gratification deferral.

As your saver begins to earn toward their objective, help motivate them by providing an additional monetary incentive for a rapid goal attainment. You can do this by adding another $10 to the account if they attain a certain savings objective by a certain date. Watch them throughout the week and provide them with a high degree of support and encouragement in their efforts. At the end of each week, take the savings check from them and staple it to their savings agreement. As they reach their goal, reinforce the positive differences between saving and borrowing. Help them understand that both concepts have their place in life, and both are important to understand.

Chapter Challenge ....

Depending on the age and developmental levels of your children, select one of the two scenarios outlined in this chapter. Younger children will benefit from visiting the arcade while older ones will benefit from the borrowing exercise. Eventually younger children will participate in the borrowing exercise, and both younger and older children should work up to the savings agreement example. Use the borrowing and savings examples regularly, and make sure your children develop a sense of borrowing responsibility as well as a savings sense.

....

....

CHAPTER 37

The Four Family Savings Accounts

*Even if you're on the right track, you'll get run over
if you just sit there.*

—WILL ROGERS

BY SPENDING TIME WITH YOUR YOUNG SAVERS AND HELPING them structure a plan to attain the goals they have set for themselves, you have enabled them to get a taste of real-world success activity. If you were to look around and observe those among us who have truly attained financial independence, you'll notice that they all have a strong propensity to save and invest.

Borrowing is something your children may do out of necessity to take advantage of an opportunity, but their overall focus ought to be oriented toward savings and accumulation. I have outlined a number of strategies for you to use with your children to help them become savings based. Through the exercises, you have shown them the benefits and drawbacks to borrowing and the advantages of a structured savings plan. After these two examples, it is hoped that they have made the decision to focus on the savings agreement rather than the note as a way to attain the things they desire.

As parents, we must understand that we set an example every day. Everything we do is monitored by the occupants of our homes. If we are advocating a certain type of behavior for our children, we ought to adopt that same behavior ourselves. I touched on personal financial responsibility briefly when I discussed budgeting several chapters ago. You'll recall we implemented a personal debt elimination plan through a basic budget model. By this time I hope that you've shredded your unnecessary credit cards and are working diligently to eliminate all unsecured and revolving debt.

You should be thinking about and taking action to establish an emergency fund as well as a retirement fund and college savings accounts for your children. Basically, as the head of the household, you should save actively through four separate personal savings accounts. These accounts should be established for, in order of importance, your emergency fund, your retirement fund, your college savings fund, and your family goal fund. Let's look at each one separately.

Your Emergency Fund

The emergency fund is perhaps the most important layer of protection and safety you can provide for the immediate needs of your family. By establishing this fund, you ensure that if anything were to happen to the primary or secondary source of income for the family, the family's basic needs would be met for a specific period of time. Initially, as a minimum, this should be an amount to cover a one month's budget. As you develop your savings abilities, you'll want to increase this to three, four, and eventually six months of budgeted expenses. If anything were to happen, you could rest assured that you have at least six months to get back on your feet again. As you learn to save, you'll find that the size of your emergency fund will be in direct proportion to the amount of financial peace that is enjoyed in your home.

Your Retirement Fund

For most of us, the retirement fund is our first and most active form of savings. Many employers offer their employees some form of payroll deduction toward a retirement account. These plans could be in the form of a defined benefit plan, defined contribution plan, 401(k), or employee stock ownership plan (ESOP). Whatever your options may be, if you've eliminated your personal credit card debt and have at least a thirty-day emergency fund, you should maximize your contributions to these retirements savings vehicles. The tax benefits derived through these qualified plans will add tremendously to your accumulation potential. It is tough to generate an after-tax yield that will exceed the performance of your retirement vehicle.

If you haven't paid off your credit cards yet, do that first before you get carried away with your retirement account. The math is quite simple; the 18% guaranteed interest charge on a credit card is substantially greater than any other guaranteed rate you can earn on an investment in a retirement savings plan. What we're talking about here is the game of net cash flow, and you are either winning or losing. A credit card that charges 18% will hurt your cash flow more than most investments will help it. Pay off your credit cards first and then start socking it away for the golden years. If you don't, you'll wind up with the rusted years instead.

Your College Savings Fund(s)

After you've paid off all your unsecured debt, established an emergency fund for at least thirty days, and established deposits to your retirement account, it is time to establish your children's college savings accounts.

According to recent College Board statistics, the estimated average expense for four years at a public school is around $40,000. The estimated average expense for four years at a private school is around $86,000. Figure 37-1 illustrates the monthly savings amounts that are necessary to fully fund a college savings account for both a public and a private education. You'd better have a seat.

Before you throw this book down or get too discouraged, remember that parents, on average, fund only about one-third of their children's education. The rest usually comes from grants, scholarships, and financial aid. If you're like the rest of us, we're still working on our emergency fund, so don't get frustrated. As long as you have the information at your disposal, you can be proactive and take the first steps toward establishing your emergency, retirement, and college funds.

Your Family Goal Fund

While you may feel a bit overwhelmed concerning the establishment of a retirement or college fund, you still can have some fun and set a great example for your children through the family goal fund. This separate savings project will serve as the family's goal reminder sheet objective. With this account, you can set an easily attainable family objective, such as a short vacation, a backyard playscape, or a well-used family watercraft.

The great thing about a family goal fund is that you can use a piggy-bank type savings vehicle for the accumulation. There's nothing like seeing a pile of money accumulate toward a specific family objective. As your family begins to accumulate funds toward your common goal, everyone will want to pitch in their spare change or a spare dollar. After this amount grows for a while, you'll want to establish a bank account for the fund. Dump the big dollars into the account and continue to accumulate at home. Before long, you'll be vacationing in the sand or swinging from your playscape, or skiing behind your new used boat.

By establishing a common objective that would be fun for the entire family, you can make tangible the goal attainment process. Figure 37-2 is an example of the family goal sheet. Through this sheet, you can set a family objective, a time frame within which

FIGURE 37-1

COLLEGE SAVINGS REQUIREMENTS
(Monthly Deposit)

Assumptions:

1. College costs will grow at 7% annually.
2. Four-year public school costs are $40,000 in 1999.
3. Four-year private school costs are $86,000 in 1999.
4. Return on investment is compounded monthly.
5. No college savings exist to date.

PUBLIC COLLEGE EDUCATION

YEARS UNTIL COLLEGE	ANNUAL RETURN ON INVESTMENT			
	6%	8%	10%	12%
2	1,446	1,418	1,391	1,364
4	782	750	720	691
6	562	528	495	464
8	455	417	382	349
10	392	351	313	279
12	351	307	267	231
14	324	276	233	196
16	304	252	207	169
18	290	234	187	148

PRIVATE COLLEGE EDUCATION

YEARS UNTIL COLLEGE	ANNUAL RETURN ON INVESTMENT			
	6%	8%	10%	12%
2	3,390	3,325	3,260	3,197
4	1,832	1,759	1,688	1,619
6	1,319	1,238	1,162	1,088
8	1,067	979	896	819
10	919	823	735	655
12	824	720	626	543
14	759	646	547	461
16	713	591	487	398
18	680	548	438	347

you will attain the objective, a weekly or monthly savings commitment, and a graphic representation of your goal attainment time line. Each of these four components is essential to the family goal attainment process.

As you can see, the goal attainment time line provides a very helpful graphic representation of the goal project's actual progress. This visual representation helps motivate family members to participate in the family goal attainment process. The family goal sheet can also be found on KPM.com by printing out Form FGS-1.

Right now it doesn't matter whether you have an emergency fund or not. It doesn't matter how much you have in your IRA or 401(k). It doesn't matter if you've already funded your children's college accounts or whether you have a family goal project. What does matter is that you have the knowledge and a new sense of

FIGURE 37-2

FAMILY GOAL SHEET

Today's Date: _____

Family Motto: _____

Our Goal Is: _____

Dollars Needed: $ _____

Dollars Saved: $ _____

We Want to Reach Our Goal By: _____

START |--------|--------|--------|--------|--------| GOAL
       20%   40%   60%   80%   100% ATTAINED

My interest is in the future, because I'm going to be
spending the rest of my life there.
—CHARLES KETTERING

commitment. You have made the determination to eliminate your debt, and you are motivated to do better and establish a few different savings vehicles for your family. Even if you put in just $10 a month split four ways, you're still making progress. Although $10 doesn't sound like a lot, it's $10 more than if you didn't make the commitment.

Make the decision to start *now*. It's not as much the amount you save as it is the fact that you are establishing a savings habit. By setting aside a few dollars each check now, you set the precedent for larger contributions at a later date. Every journey begins with the first step. Why not take that step right now?

Chapter Challenge ....

The easiest, most visible, and most attainable account you can establish is the family goal account. Talk with your family and decide on a family goal that can be attained within the next six to eight weeks. Whether it's a small vacation, a family toy, or a new pet, set a family goal and fill out your family goal sheet. Obtain a clear container and write "Family Goal Fund" on the outside. Start your journey and deposit a few dollars in the container. Discuss the excitement of your family goal attainment and visualize it happening. Write the results in your family journal.

....

CHAPTER 38

Financial Success Journal

*The great thing about getting older is that you don't
lose all the other ages you've been.*

—MADELEINE L'ENGLE

OVER THE COURSE OF THIS BOOK, YOU HAVE BEEN RECORDING A
lot of information in your family journal: results of family meetings, personal achievements, different goals you have set for yourselves, and a number of experiences you've had with family members.

This record will serve as a bit of a family history. As you maintain the journal, entering significant and even less than significant events into it, you will be writing a history that you can look back on and cherish. As your children grow, change, and mature, their entries will be especially valuable. Documenting the things they have done and the things they have said will become a priceless piece of your family's history.

As events are entered into the family journal, experience will promote personal growth and development, which will become evident in the journal entries. As you review earlier entries, you'll see how attitudes and personal habits have changed. Often mistakes that are made and lessons that are learned will become valuable references for future consideration. Younger siblings can

read the experiences of older children to gain a sense of cama-
raderie. "You mean that you went through this too?" will be a
common response as the younger children read about the family
events of yesterday.

Successes and achievements also can be documented to be
reflected upon. Many times we get caught up in the daily grind
and forget about some of the good things we've done in the past.
Reviewing records of these positive events can serve as a personal
therapy of sorts and will take the edge off of any self-depreciating
tendencies we may have as challenged parents and spouses.

The benefits of keeping a family journal are great in number
and significance. By having a record to review, our personal
mission and direction will quickly return to focus, and we'll eliminate any self-doubt we may have about what we are doing and
whether the effort we expend maintaining family relationships is
worth it.

As our family grows and develops, so too does our personal
financial condition. Just as a family journal helps us maintain a
degree of personal clarity, a financial journal will help us maintain financial clarity. By keeping a written record of all our financial decisions and positions, we enable ourselves to look
objectively on our situation and evaluate whether we are making
the right financial decisions. We also have a record of past deal-
ings and their outcomes for future reference.

A good financial journal will have four basic components:
opportunities, assets, liabilities, and the net worth snapshot. Each
component should be maintained as a separate section of the
journal and updated at least monthly. Let's take a look at each
area.

Opportunities

The opportunities section represents the ability to document all
the employment and investment options that come your way. You
will, from time to time, be presented with various opportunities

to participate in activities and investments that offer the chance at gain. These opportunities could come in the form of a new career option, a business investment, a land investment, or an opportunity through an investment broker. Whatever the source of the opportunity, by writing down the pertinent facts, you will gain a clearer understanding of the options available to you. Also, by writing down the characteristics of the deal, you give yourself the chance to better understand the details of what is being offered. The more you understand something, the greater the chance you'll make the right decision about the issue. By taking the time to write down the details, you give yourself the chance to take some time with the decision. Never make a hasty decision regarding an opportunity. Chances are that if it needs to be acted on at that instant, the possibility of instant decline is as great as instant appreciation. Be careful with the you-gotta-decide-it-now opportunities.

Another benefit to writing down the opportunities that come your way is that you can begin to develop a track record of the various sources that are bringing the deals to you. If you're dealing with a broker who makes a number of suggestions regularly, you can easily keep tabs on the suggestions and their performance. If you deal with a number of brokers, you'll quickly see the cream rise to the top through consistent performance of their suggested investments.

By creating a detailed documentation of your opportunity characteristics and then outlining your decisions about those opportunities, you'll generate trend information about yourself that will be indispensable. If you track your own decision performance, you'll quickly see your strengths and weaknesses emerge. In attempting to identify these personal characteristics, you'll become better able to evaluate opportunities as they relate to your personal capabilities. To establish this level of objectivity for yourself, your chances of making a bad decision will decrease steadily over time.

Assets

Keeping track of what you own is an important element of creating financial success through your financial journal. You should keep track not only of what you own but also of how those assets are performing for you.

List everything you own in your assets section. Some of the software programs like Microsoft Money or Intuit's Quicken will help you detail your assets. As a rule, you'll want to itemize everything that cost over $100 when you purchased it. This list will help you evaluate your purchasing habits as well as the value performance of the things you buy. If you spend a lot of money on new automobiles, for example, you'll find out that you're losing a big percentage of your investment to depreciation. If you spend your money on investments or collectibles, you'll see the opposite happen. No matter what you buy, you'll see the results of your decisions over time in the assets section of your financial journal.

Liabilities

It is hoped that the liabilities section will be the smallest and least used section of your financial journal. Any time you borrow money through a credit card, loan, or mortgage, you need to document the decision in this section. Along with the name of the creditor, document how much was borrowed, for what purpose, the terms of the contract, any collateral, and the interest rate. You'll also want to calculate roughly what the credit will cost you by multiplying the loan amount by the interest rate by the number of years. Don't forget to reduce the principal by the annual payment amount to calculate subsequent annual finance charges.

Net Worth Snapshot

The net worth snapshot section should be the most fun for you to maintain because it represents your lifetime financial achievement bottom line and reflects everything you have done with your finances. The rate at which this figure changes will illustrate the effectiveness of your financial decision making.

The net worth snapshot should be recalculated at least quarterly or as often as monthly, depending on your rate of change. You can calculate the figure easily by subtracting your total liabilities from your total assets. If you've been working in the same occupation for a while, the bottom number should be growing at a steady pace. If you're an entrepreneur just starting out, the number is likely to be negative and falling. If you've inherited a great deal of wealth, you've probably got an accountant who prepares your financial statements and you've skipped this section completely.

Whatever your status may be, it's always good to have a clear picture of your financial condition, including your assets, liabilities, and net worth. How you handle the opportunities that come your way can provide you with an insight of tremendous value. Knowing your own financial strengths and weaknesses will be beneficial throughout your lifetime. By developing a clear understanding of where you are today, you'll be able to map out a detailed course of action that will get you where you want to be tomorrow.

If you have a personal computer at home or in your office, you may want to investigate some of the personal financial software that is available. I use Intuit's Quicken program. Through Quicken, I am able to track all of the information discussed in this chapter. The net worth calculation is accomplished with the click of a button, and you can monitor your daily progress. There's nothing quite like watching your personal net worth increase as a result of applied financial intelligence.

Chapter Challenge ....

Review your family journal and make sure that you are fully utilizing your resources to your benefit. Begin a financial journal and include sections on opportunity, assets, liabilities, and the net worth snapshot. Conduct a personal inventory to develop those sections. Calculate your current net worth, and document your most recent opportunity, whether it was at work, an investment, or in business. If you have a personal computer, make sure you are using a personal financial package to monitor your progress.

....

··

CHAPTER 39

Stocks, Bonds, and Mutual Funds

Nothing is worth more than this day.

—JOHANN W. VON GOETHE

INVESTMENT AND SAVING REPRESENT TWO DISTINCTLY DIFFERENT methods of capital management. Saving implies the ability to systematically deposit funds into an account in order to accumulate an amount sufficient to meet a predetermined objective. Resources are typically saved at little or no risk and earn a commensurate return during the accumulation process. Usually savings rates are based on inflation. A passbook savings account essentially guarantees a small loss in purchasing power while funds are held in the account.

Many individuals don't understand this principle and are satisfied to use a passbook savings to accumulate net worth slowly. The interest rate you'll earn on a savings account is the lowest rate at which your banker can borrow money from you. For example, if you deposit $10,000 into a savings account, you may earn as low as 2.5% on that account while you keep your money there. This means that the banker will pay you approximately $250 a year for the privilege of using your money.

Contrary to what most people think, the banker doesn't put the cash in a vault for safekeeping until you need it again. The banker usually lends the funds to someone else at a higher rate of interest than their cost ($250). This means that the banker will take your money and lend it to your next-door neighbors for 10.25% so they can buy their new car. The bank will earn $1,025 on the loan, pay you the $250, and profit $775 on your deposit. It's no wonder that banks own the biggest buildings in all the major cities around the country.

You can make other bank deposits if you're looking for more interest than a current savings rate. Certificates of deposit (CDs) enable you to earn a higher rate if you're willing to commit your funds for a predetermined period of time. The banker will pay you more for your money if you guarantee that you won't touch the deposit for a specified period. For consideration of your guarantee, your banker will add on another 2 or 3% and secure up your deposit from six to forty-eight months. Those extra few percentage points represent your banker's time value of money. Even at the highest rates offered on the longest-term CD, you will still only match or slightly beat inflation. By keeping your savings in a bank, all you do is retain your purchasing power and provide your banker additional funds to lend out at higher rates.

One of the major benefits to keeping your money in a bank however, is that the funds are FDIC insured. What that means is that if your bank fails, the Federal Deposit Insurance Corporation will repay you, the depositor, up to $100,000 per account. If you have an account that has more than $100,000 in it, you'll only get the $100,000 back that is insured.

Bankers collect deposits from savers and then lend those funds out to borrowers; as middlemen they can earn a handsome reward. When I was a broker, I helped my clients bypass the middleman and lend their funds directly to borrowers. The investment vehicle that enabled my clients to accomplish this is called a bond.

A bond is simply a tool that allows a corporation or government to borrow funds from individual or corporate investors. Bonds have a stated interest rate, a maturity date, and a credit rating. The combination of these three factors will determine the relative risk of the investment to the investor and the bond's current yield.

Just like certificates of deposit, the longer the maturity date, the higher the interest the bond will pay. And just like at the bank, the lower the credit rating, the higher the interest the borrower (bond issuer) will have to pay. Credit ratings on bonds are given by two sources, Moody's and Standard & Poor's. Each independent rating agency considers a number of factors in determining a bond's credit rating including the issuer's financial strength, the issuer's industry, and whether the bond is insured or not.

Bonds are considered fixed income securities and are suitable for investors who are looking for income rather than capital gain. A bond represents the closest comparable investment to a bank certificate of deposit and gives investors the opportunity to lend their money directly to the borrower and bypass the banker as a middleman. The corporations, utilities, and governments that issue bonds are usually mature organizations that need capital to purchase high-cost plant and equipment resources.

Bonds will pay an interest rate that is commensurate with their credit rating and length of time to maturity. A typical corporate bond usually pays a rate that yields approximately 40% more than bank certificates of deposit of comparable maturity. Bonds pay interest semiannually.

Bonds are bought and sold on the open market, and their prices usually fluctuate with the overall prevailing interest rates. If interest rates in general are going up, bond prices go down. If interest rates are going down, bond prices go up. Bonds usually are callable at a certain price on a certain date. Callable means that the issuer (the company issuing the bond) has the option to buy back the bond under certain, prespecified conditions. If you own a bond that is callable, and interest rates are lower than when the bond was issued, the bond probably will be called. Your bond will be paid off because the issuer can issue new bonds at a lower interest rate and use those funds to pay off your older bonds that have a higher interest rate.

Another fixed income security available is called a preferred stock. This investment represents a preferred equity interest in a company that will pay a relatively high stated dividend to the stock owner. By purchasing a preferred stock, an investor can enjoy a high-yielding dividend for income and at the same time share in the success of the company through an equity participation. Preferred stock carries a fixed dividend that usually pays quarterly. The preferred stock trades more like a bond than a stock, however. It has a stated par value (usually $25 per share), a stated dividend yield, and usually a predetermined call date. The call date on a preferred stock is simply the date whereby the issuer can call in any outstanding shares by paying the stated par value or par value with a slight premium. Because of the call dates and the stated dividend on preferred stock, the price volatility is relatively low on these shares. Just like bonds, preferred stock will provide investors with an excellent high-yield alternative to bank certificates of deposit.

When I was a broker, however, I rarely suggested individual bonds or preferred stock to my clients. Buying only one issue from a single company does not provide investors with the necessary and appropriate diversification. Instead, I would recommend a fixed income mutual fund that could provide not only a competitive dividend yield but also an inherent diversification with professional management. Fixed income mutual funds typically pay their dividends monthly and usually offer a dividend reinvestment option. The mutual fund concept provides investors with a quality resource for both fixed income and equity investing across a broad spectrum of industries and objectives.

Mutual funds are used by the majority of 401(k) plans. By offering diversification, professional management, and simplicity of the mutual fund for retirement investing, the 401(k) enables plan participants to maximize their retirement investment performance. All plan participants can customize their plan portfolios for their needs and objectives without having to spend a great deal of time managing the account.

Another excellent investment vehicle to use as an alternative to bank saving or certificates of deposit is called the money market mutual fund. This fund is an investment portfolio of short-term federally insured government investments. It is highly liquid and provides an investment resource similar to a savings account but with twice the yield. Most banks and brokerage accounts have a money market fund option available for noninvested cash assets.

There are only a couple of drawbacks to investing in mutual funds. One is that most funds you purchase through a stockbroker will carry a fee or commission. These rates will be anywhere from 1 to 8.5% depending on the fund and amount deposited. Typically, the more you invest at one time or can commit over a year, the lower the commission. The fund managers also charge annual management fees. The managers are the people who actually make the fund's investment decisions and are the ones responsible for the fund's performance. The annual management fee is typically between 1 and 2% and will be deducted from the fund's net asset value (NAV) during the year.

No-load funds available through discount brokerage houses and from the funds themselves offer a low-cost alternative to your local stockbroker. If you have the knowledge necessary to make your own investment and market decisions, you will save a few dollars by going it alone with the no-load funds. If you are looking for some guidance or expertise, you're probably better off paying a few percent up front for professional advice. Every no-load fund has an annual management fee that is deducted from the NAV.

A slight drawback to mutual fund investing is that performance will be limited to the average investment performance within the portfolio. What this means is that the larger the fund, the more difficult it is for the manager to maintain performance. Mutual funds are a lot like boats; the bigger they are, the less maneuverable they are. If you've invested in a multibillion-dollar mutual fund, the managers have their hands full watching over such a large portfolio and can be challenged to make a meaningful gain. This fund is analogous to an ocean liner. Likewise, if you put your money in a small aggressive fund of less than several hundred million dollars, the manager has the opportunity to maneuver the fund tactically and exploit various opportunities that may appear. This fund is like a power boat.

To further our analogy, the captains of these vessels (the fund managers) will have experience commensurate with the size of their boat. Typically, large-fund managers are the most experienced captains around and have the wherewithal to weather almost any storm. Small-fund managers are the charter boat captains operating in their own maneuverable crafts in their own familiar waters.

Mutual funds provide the novice investor with an opportunity to participate in a variety of different markets and investment types. No better vehicles are available to learn the basic principles of investing. By analyzing mutual fund annual reports and sales material, you will gain an insight into the fund's management and performance. By learning how the fund is managed and becoming familiar with investment terminology, you can prepare yourself to make some individual investment decisions at a later date. By watching a fund's NAV, you will become familiar with the fund's performance and overall movement of its investment sector and market.

If you are watching a general equity fund, as you observe the movement, you'll begin to see some similarities between fund prices and stock market activity in general. This is because most equity funds are comprised of many of the same stocks that make up the broader market index.

After a period of time watching the market's movement, you

will soon learn about the investor's guarantee, the only guarantee any investment ever provides. This universal guarantee, which applies to all investments, whether stock, bond, mutual fund, insured, or junk rated, assures investors of one unchangeable fact: All investments, no matter what other conditions may apply, will fluctuate in value.

Market fluctuation accounts for all the stress, pain, suffering, profit, and excitement of the investment experience. Those who are experienced in the market have learned to overlook market volatility and focus on their long-term investment objectives.

The most speculative investor will buy a security with the hopes that the value will go up over a very short period of time. Some traders even buy in the morning and sell the same security in the afternoon. This technique is called day trading and it's becoming more popular than ever. Day traders are growing in numbers, primarily due to the Internet. Internet access allows anyone with a few dollars in an account to go online and roll the dice in the market of choice. The difference between the experienced investment professional and the day trader is essentially the difference between investing and gambling. If you want to roll the dice and have a little excitement and quite possibly make some money, open an Internet brokerage account and give it a whirl. If, on the other hand, you want to establish a long-term capital gain objective and map out a plan for its attainment, read on.

Chapter Challenge ....

Visit your local bookstore or library and review issues of *Money, Fortune, Forbes,* and *Kiplinger's.* By taking the time to understand how these periodicals are put together, you'll gain an insight into which financial publication best suits your needs. You should also buy a copy of the *Investor's Business Daily* and consider a subscription; it's one of the best sources of up-to-date financial information you'll find anywhere.

....

CHAPTER 40

....

The Investment
Process

Chance favors the prepared mind.

—LOUIS PASTEUR

JUST AS WE'VE BEEN WORKING WITH OUR CHILDREN TO TEACH them basic financial principles, we can apply the same logical discipline to our own investment thinking. What have been the key points throughout this book? Set a goal, define responsibilities, look for opportunity, defer gratification, and attain the goal. Let's take a look at how these principles apply to our own investment decisions.

1. Set a Goal

We first need to know where we are before we can plot a course to where we want to go. If you completed the challenge in chapter 38, you've got a pretty good idea of where you are today. If you haven't completed that challenge, I suggest you do so now before continuing.

Now that you know where you are financially, specifically your investment assets, you'll need to figure out where you want to go. By setting an objective for yourself, you will add a degree of focus and discipline to your investment process. Your goal may be to beat the Standard & Poor's 500 index or to gain 15% over the next twelve months. Whatever your objective is, by knowing it, you can achieve it. If you have no goal, you have no measure.

2. Define Responsibilities

Just as your children understand their responsibilities within your home, you'll want to establish certain guidelines for your investment process. As a broker, I often helped my clients establish portfolio objectives and limits.

One of the rules I usually suggested had to do with their asset allocation model. Asset allocation is how you spread out your portfolio among fixed income, equity, and cash investments. Traditionally, the older you are, the more fixed income securities you should own as a percentage of your total portfolio. A good rule of thumb is 100 minus your age equals the cash and equity component percentage of your portfolio. If you are forty-five years old, fifty-five percent of your portfolio should be allocated to equity and cash securities. The reasoning behind this is that the older you are, the less risk you can take and the more income you may need to supplement the loss of wages after retirement.

Another helpful rule to follow in mutual fund investing is to try to stay within the same mutual fund family. You'll want to do this because mutual fund commissions are based on total dollars invested. Commission breakpoints (the point at which the commission amount is reduced) usually occur at $10,000, $25,000, $50,000, and $100,000. These breakpoints apply to the total investment within a family of funds, not a specific fund.

If you decide to buy individual stocks, you should commit up front to a long-term investment strategy instead of watching prices daily. The odd-lot theory says that investors typically decide to do exactly the opposite of what they should do with their investments. When the price of an investment goes down, investors want to sell. When the price of an investment goes up, they always want to buy more. Unseasoned investors who do this are actually buying high and selling low, exactly opposite of the buy-low-and-sell-high adage. These investors are truly an odd lot.

Experienced investors understand the theory of relative value per share. Relative value per share is analogous to a share's price to earnings ratio. If the price of a stock goes down, its value per share goes up. If the price of a portfolio stock decreases, the relative value per share is higher and more shares should be purchased at the lower price. Conversely, if the price of a portfolio stock increases, the relative value per share goes down. This may be a good opportunity to capture a gain, wait for the price to come back down, and buy more shares, exactly opposite of what a typical investor's emotions will dictate.

3. Look for Opportunity

If you are investing in mutual funds, a lot of the due diligence work is taken out of the investment process for you. Funds have professional managers who can invest fund resources much more effectively than any day trader or market timer. If you've decided to use mutual funds as your vehicle of choice, any good financial publication lists the top performers. Most of the majors list the best performing funds in order of growth in their various segments.

A key statistic for you to consider is the fund's five- or ten-year average performance. Any fund can have a super last twelve months, but it takes some talent to stay at the top consistently. Look for the funds with the best five- and ten-year numbers, and make sure the management has stayed the same. If you find a fund with good long-term performance and solid established management, it may be the one for you. Remember, however, past performance is no guarantee of future performance.

If you decide to try your hand at picking individual stocks, make sure you do your homework and research your picks thoroughly. Try to spend as much energy researching your investment as it took you to earn the money you're about to invest. Remember, *Investor's Business Daily* is an excellent daily research guide. It's a very popular resource for market information and is used by many financial professionals for research and stock selection.

As you review the information on your potential mutual fund, stock, or bond investment, you'll quickly find that there is no shortage of investment opportunity out there. Your level of success will be determined by what you choose to put your money in and then how long you choose to keep it there.

4. Defer Gratification

Just as our children need to learn to save for their goal items and control their spending, we as investors need to understand the importance of buying an investment and holding on to it. Most of the extraordinary money managers have gained their reputations by first picking great investments and then by holding them for a long period of time. The discipline of being able to buy and hold the right securities is the difference between the successful investor and ordinary stock traders.

One of the greatest habits you can develop is the ability to buy and hold an investment. The long-term growth you will experience through a disciplined investment strategy will far outweigh any timing or luck you may have by moving quickly in and out of stock positions. Every time you change your mind about an investment, you open yourself up to the chance that you'll buy into a risky company.

When you are buying a particular stock, get to know and understand the company. Spend time reviewing the annual report, and look on the Internet for any pertinent information. You'll be able to acquire general company research from a variety of Web sources. Two of my favorites are www.pcquote.com and www.investors.com. Both sites provide a great variety of investment information and up-to-date market and economic information. While you're on www.investors.com, make sure you review their Investment Education Course; it's a great information resource.

If you're inclined to dig deeper into a company before you invest, you may want to visit its Internet site to review its annual and quarterly reports and federal filings. You should go into this depth of research any time you decide to invest in a specific company's stock.

As you hold stock in a company, you'll gain an intimate understanding of the company's performance and objectives. This kind of detailed knowledge is what earns you the right to share in the gains of the company. Flipping in and out of positions trying to catch the next big move is a risky way to handle your future life support system.

5. Attain the Goal

Keep track of your investing performance as your experience accumulates. If your aim was to beat the S&P 500 over a certain period of time, did you do it? If you wanted to have a capital appreciation of 15% over the last twelve months, did you? Hold yourself accountable to your goals. If you attain your goals, reward yourself and also take a minute to analyze your goal attainment process. Can you do it again? Can you do better? Does your next goal need to be more challenging? These self-evaluation questions are important to your continued success as an investor; make sure you stay challenged.

By now you and your children are beginning to have some great conversations and financial experiences through the chapter challenge ideas. As you gain confidence and learn to invest for yourself, you'll want to help your children obtain a like understanding of the markets and share in your increased knowledge. There are a number of ways you can accomplish this through the Internet and at home.

A number of Internet resources will be helpful for your children to learn about investing and money basics. By going to KPM.com, you'll find links to all of the sites listed below. Next time you're online with your kids, you may want to check out:

www.pocketcard.com

www.jumpstartcoalition.org

www.talks.com/library/nd112995.html

www.moneyopolis.com

www.icanbuy.com

www.library.advanced.org/3096/index.htm

www.smithbarney.com/yin/

www.sec.gov/consumer/camp99/quiz.htm

www.ssa.gov/kids/

www.kidsbank.com

www.strongkids.com

www.treas.gov/kids/

www.ici.org/aboutfunds/addl_resources_young.html

www.coolbank.com

www.fleetkids.com

www.smg2000.org

www.youngmoney.com

www.kidsmoneycents.com

www.younginvestor.com/home.shtml

www.mainxchange.com/stockgame/

www.rlig.com

www.plan.ml.com/family/kids

www.naf-education.org/finance/finind.html

www.better-investing.org/youth/

www.ncfe.org/catalog/cat.html

www.nefe.org/

www.nice.emich.edu/

www.kidstock.com/en/default.asp

www.kidsmoneystore.com

www.investoreducation.org/cindex.htm

www.asec.org/youthsurvey.pdf

www.wa.gov/ago/youth

www.consumerfed.org/teachchild.pdf

www.youngnbiz.com

www.studentcredit.com

www.girlsinc.org (click on "tips for parents")

www.nationalcouncil.org

www.americanexpress.com/advisors/advice/education/kids.asp

www.pueblo.gsa.gov/children.htm

www.allowancenet.com

www.kidsmoney.org

www.sos.state.il.us/depts/securities/begin.html

www.wisepockets.com

These sites provide fun and exciting ways for your kids to learn about money and investing basics. Some of the portfolio games may be enjoyable for you as well. Spend time with your children to help them learn about the more sophisticated principles of investing; through this experience they will gain an understanding of the importance of the basic money skills learned around your home.

By now your children should begin to see the life-size financial picture that has been painted through their home-based financial experiences. Once they can comprehend the full-circle effects of personal financial literacy and responsibility, they'll be prepared and motivated to be proactive and willing contributors to society.

As your children learn about the benefits and security provided by financial intelligence, they will be motivated to design and execute their own personal financial plan. Through financial intelligence they will have the necessary tools to capture a life's vision, design a vision attainment process, execute their plan, and self-monitor the long distance to ultimate success. Young adults who possess these skills are complete in their preparation to live life to its fullest.

Chapter Challenge ....

Sit down with your children and get on the Internet together. Go to www.kidsparentsandmoney.com and review some of the sites listed. Play the stock market game at www.younginvestor.com. Take a moment to review the five steps listed in this chapter. Let your children know that the financial lessons they have been learning at home will apply to them throughout their lives. Record in your journal any notable comments your children make throughout this exercise.

If you haven't already done so, visit PocketCard through KPM.com. This debit card will give your kids an awesome tool to apply the lessons they are learning here.

CHAPTER 41

Publicly Traded Securities

I've found that luck is quite predictable. If you want more
luck, take more chances. Be more active. Show up more often.

—BRIAN TRACY

THE LAST CHAPTER PROVIDED A VERY BROAD OVERVIEW OF THE
investment process and how that process may pertain to your
overall financial objectives. This chapter deals with a more detailed
analysis of those companies that make up the overall market.

If it hasn't happened already, eventually you will find yourself
in a situation where a friend or broker presents you with a "hot"
tip on a company that is getting ready to break through the stratosphere. When this happens, you'll want to be familiar with some
of the most basic principles of investment analysis so you don't
get into too much trouble betting the farm on a long shot. Most
investors are content to let a qualified investment consultant
make recommendations regarding the opportunities that present
themselves, but you would do well to understand the basics of
what makes up a good investment opportunity.

The best policy for any investment strategy is to buy and hold.
The chances of hitting the big time on one investment are
extremely low. Most successful (and very wealthy) investors own
stocks that have appreciated greatly over an *extended* period

of time. Those fortunate enough to get in early on Dell or anythingbigontheInternet.com are excluded. Even then, if investors bought Dell or .com early and got an itchy profit trigger finger, they're kicking themselves right now for selling early. When you make it a personal policy to buy and hold, you can take the emotion out of your investing and sleep well at night. Remember, there are old investors and there are bold investors, but there are very few old bold investors.

When you make the determination to buy stock and hold on to it, investment research and analysis take on new significance. Knowing what to look for will shorten your due diligence time as well as add a high degree of confidence in your selections. Basing an investment decision on a preselected set of facts and statistical information will ensure that you don't compromise your investing integrity on the emotion of a hot tip.

Before getting started on stock analysis and investment strategy, it would be good to review a few key pieces of information about the market itself. Understanding the different exchanges and what the various indexes represent will give you a basic foundation of investment knowledge on which you can build.

Stocks are traded daily on two major markets, "registered exchanges" and "over the counter" (OTC). These markets are like any other market you would visit as a place where buyers and sellers can meet. Instead of buying and selling fruits and vegetables, these traders are busy exchanging ownership in companies through common stock.

The registered exchanges are comprised of a number of stock exchanges across the country that "make markets" in the over 4,000 "listed" issues of common stock. The requirements for a company to be listed on the registered exchanges are substantial, and only the largest and most stable companies are listed. The most notable of the registered exchanges is the "big board," the New York Stock Exchange. The NYSE is the largest and most important of the registered exchanges where over half of all

American listed trades take place. The "big board" leads the other registered stock exchanges in both daily volume and the number of issues traded.

The second-largest registered exchange is the American Stock Exchange, or AMEX, which is about half the size of the NYSE in terms of volume and numbers of listed issues. Many of the issues traded on the New York Stock Exchange are also traded on regional stock exchanges. These exchanges include:

Boston Stock Exchange

Cincinnati Stock Exchange

Midwest Stock Exchange (Chicago)

Pacific Stock Exchange (San Francisco)

Philadelphia Stock Exchange

Most of the securities trading exchanges have visitors' centers where individuals can view the activity on the trading floor. My wife and I have taken our kids to the Midwest Exchange in Chicago and had a great time. The kids were amazed that order could be maintained in what looked to be a chaotic mess on the floor. If you ever have the chance to take your children or grandchildren to an exchange, you should do so. The experience will impress upon them the reality and excitement derived from financial stability. The memories created by the visit will motivate them throughout their lives to achieve a higher financial state. If they are like my kids, they'll want to grow up and have enough financial fortitude to "get in the game" and participate themselves.

As I mentioned, the registered exchanges list over 4,000 individual companies stocks. The over-the-counter market covers over 30,000 different issues. The over-the-counter automated system allows securities brokers to trade directly with one another through the National Association of Securities Dealers Automated Quotron system (Nasdaq). The National Association of Securities

Dealers is the association to which every registered representative (stockbroker) must belong, and a Quotron is a computer screen that brokers use to monitor stocks and track market activity. Yes, Nasdaq does stand for something that makes sense.

By establishing a network between stockbrokers, the Nasdaq allows investors to trade issues of stock that are too small to be traded on a registered exchange. Historically, most stocks listed on the Nasdaq have had a relatively small following and have only limited demand from the market in general. The advent of the Internet is changing that; now a small northern California company with little or no earnings can attract global interest overnight through its Internet distribution. The next two decades are going to be an exciting and amazing time for investors, the companies they invest in, and the exchanges that effect the transactions.

When you read the paper or watch the news at night, you'll notice that the media use several indexes to report the day's trading activity. These indexes are the Dow Jones Industrial Average (DJIA), Standard & Poor's 500 "S&P 500 index," and the Nasdaq Composite Index. The Dow Jones Industrial Average is the key barometer used to measure general market activity. It is a universal indicator that can be reviewed quickly to determine the extent of either a bullish (up) or bearish (down) day. The average is just that, an average assessment of the market as a whole consisting of thirty select, large industrial companies. The components, which change occasionally, represent approximately 20% of the market value of all NYSE stocks. The DJIA is calculated by adding the closing prices of the component stocks and using a divisor that is adjusted for splits and stock dividends. The average is quoted in points instead of dollars. The S&P 500 index is a European-style, capitalization-weighted index of 500 stocks that are traded on the New York Stock Exchange, American Stock Exchange, and Nasdaq National Market. The advantage of "cap weighting" is that each company's influence on index performance is directly proportional to its relative market value.

Market capitalization weighting is simply the price per share of a company's stock times the number of shares outstanding. For example, General Motors has approximately 700 million shares outstanding. A recent price per share was $62, making market capitalization approximately $44 billion.

The Nasdaq Composite Index measures all Nasdaq domestic and non-U.S.-based common stocks listed on the Nasdaq stock market. The index is market-value weighted so each company's security affects the index in proportion to its market value. The Nasdaq Composite includes over 5,000 companies, more than most other stock market indexes. Because it's so broad, the composite is one of the most widely followed and quoted major market indexes.

As a potential investor, you can benefit from learning about these market indexes as well as becoming familiar with their movement. The more knowledge you have, the more you can relay to the next generation. The more knowledge the next generation possesses, the greater its likelihood of future economic stability and success.

I've discussed markets in very general terms; by now you should have a reasonable understanding of how they work and what they report. Now it's time to take a closer look at the common stocks that are traded on those markets. Let's examine what makes up publicly traded companies, how they are valued, and how they become publicly traded in the first place. This topic represents the heart and soul of the capital markets.

Let's start at the beginning: Where do companies come from? Unlike what we may tell our young children about babies, they don't just appear out of nowhere and they aren't delivered by a stork. The truth about companies is that they come from entrepreneurs. That's right, they come about when people with good ideas team up with people who have management experience and create a viable business. Obviously companies can be formed through mergers and acquisitions, but the raw stuff of new business is entrepreneurial.

Typically, the young management team of a new business will use any money they can get their hands on. Usually this capital comes from personal savings, equity in a home, borrowing from family and friends, and perhaps a small bank loan secured by personal assets (like a home) as collateral. This early stage is when the business foundation is created and the ideas are tested to see if they really fly. It usually isn't very long, however, until the company needs more money to grow and develop. At this point, the business typically has a pretty good start on the endeavor but isn't quite mature enough to attract any real commercial investment interest.

Enter the angel. An angel is a private investor who is willing to become involved in young start-up companies and infuse capital and experience into the endeavor. Most angels are experienced businesspeople themselves and can bring a great deal more than just money to the table. If angels decide to get involved in a new company, they probably do so based more on a feeling about the project and its management than because of any great financial numbers the project is turning out. Angels are truly heaven sent to a new company and its management. The entity is usually at a stage where it doesn't qualify for any commercial funding, the principals are out of personal resources, and the idea needs more money to develop enough to attract venture capital.

Once the angel or a number of them together decide to fund the project, they usually take an equity stake in the company as well as some form of management control. The degree of equity and control depends on the scenario, but it's usually not substantial compared to the money they put in. The reason angels will settle for a lower equity stake is that they want the company founders to retain their incentive and they realize that the project probably will require several more rounds of financing before they can receive a return on their investment. Each round of financing will dilute the founders' equity interest; they must be allowed to retain sufficient equity to make it worth their financial and time commitment.

After the angels put more gas in the tank, the company can motor down the road and develop the idea to a higher level. The next step for the company, in terms of financing, is the venture capital company. These organizations have been established to fund worthy enterprises preparatory to either acquisition by a larger company or public offering. These two alternatives are the goal of every entrepreneur who has worked through the night and into the next day on a project. The acquisition or initial public offering (IPO) is the opportunity for the entrepreneur to cash out and retire. The only way the entrepreneur will ever get there, however, is through the venture capital that will propel the project into the stratosphere.

Venture capital firms represent the link between privately held small companies and the public securities universe. The capital, connections, and management expertise the venture capital company can provide are the vital elements that become the catalyst to substantial company growth. Venture capital firms are either subsidiaries of large corporations, such as Allstate Insurance or AT&T, or the creation of wealthy businesspeople. Businesspeople who start their own venture capital firm usually have gone through a high degree of business development themselves and have benefited from an acquisition or IPO of their own. Large corporations that start venture capital firms usually invest within their industry to "incubate" companies that will ultimately benefit their own market position.

The cost of venture capital is typically quite high. The firms understand very clearly that they are the last, and most vital step, between the entrepreneur's dream and its outcome. Venture capital companies either invest as deal originators, where they take the role as a lead investor, or join a syndicate of other venture capital firms to fund a particular deal. These firms typically invest from $1 million to $50 million in any single project.

Over the last decade, as the economy has prospered, venture capital firms have raised their criteria of investment to look only at bigger and bigger deals. The rationale is that they have to spend as much time in due diligence (researching the potential investment) for a $500,000 deal as they would a $10 million deal. If the percentage return is equal between investments, the dollar return is substantially higher for the larger deal with the same amount of research time invested. This is why many small deals (less that $5 million) aren't getting looked at. There are too many opportunities out there that will generate a higher dollar return for the venture capital firm.

If the venture capital firm decides to look at a project, it will thoroughly investigate the company. This process may take from three to six months. It will review everything, from the market in which the company plans to operate to a detailed investigation of the firm's principals. Lots of money is at stake in these transactions, and the venture capitalist has a fiduciary responsibility to the firm's owners to make only the best decisions.

If the young company passes due diligence, it will receive a portion of the capital necessary to achieve their objective. If the deal is for $10 million, it may get $2.5 million up front with a benchmark expectation to meet before more capital is infused. The young company probably will get a few new board members as a result of the transaction as well. These board seats will ensure that the venture capital is spent wisely and that appropriate management decisions are being made for the company.

Over time, as the venture capital is infused, the growth rate of the company will accelerate. The additional capital will allow the company to develop new products or services, open new markets, hire greater talent, and gain greater market and media share. All of these elements are necessary to attract the attention of an investment banker. The banker is the representative of the financial entity that can facilitate the next step of business evolution for the company, its founders, its angels, and its venture capital investors. The banker is the one who has the knowledge, experience, and contacts that can orchestrate an acquisition or public offering for the company.

An investment banker will become involved with an organization once it meets the necessary criteria to be acquired by a larger firm or is positioned to have its stock ownership offered to the public. Both investment bankers and venture capital companies do merger and acquisition (M&A) work. An acquisition would take place after a related firm determines that the growth company fits its needs to either open up a new market or expand an existing one. Either way, the acquiring company needs to determine that the to-be-acquired company benefits its shareholders. Once this determination is made, the acquiring company conducts its own due diligence process to check for skeletons in the closet. If none are found, the acquisition moves forward.

Usually an acquiring firm will offer the principals and investors a combination of cash and equity in the acquiring company. The percentages and deal structure will be different for every case, but the end result is the same. Finally, after years of long hours, months of having no money, and huge amounts of personal and business stress, the company founders can cash out and reap their rewards.

In most cases, the entrepreneurs' blood hasn't changed and they'll look for the next opportunity. By using the proceeds of their own company's acquisition, they can now leverage their capital and experience for the benefit of new entrepreneurs who have other great ideas. In this world there is no short supply of ideas, only capital. Entrepreneurs who have persevered unto acquisition will reap lifelong benefits from their diligence and experience.

In the case of an initial public offering, the course of events is a little different. Once the investment banker has determined that the young company meets all criteria for public ownership and due diligence is done, an underwriting syndicate must be created. This syndicate is a group of investment houses that will agree to support the initial public offering of the new company's stock. The syndicate will have a lead investor to organize the offering as well as subordinate members who will make commitments to sell a predetermined amount of the company's stock. The lead investor will prepare a prospectus that outlines all the risk factors of the company to be offered as well as other pertinent corporate information. The syndicate will receive a number of the prospectuses so that its brokers can go to work selling the offering. Typically, institutional commitment is a must if the offering is to succeed. This means that mutual funds, insurance companies, banks, and pension fund managers must have a sufficient interest in the deal and make subsequent commitments to buy shares if the offering is to succeed. Without institutional support, most offerings will fail; if they do succeed, they will be weakly traded without the institutional market price support.

Once the syndicate has been established, the principals of the company will conduct a "dog and pony" show of syndicate member firms to tell their story about what they're doing. The road show will last a number of weeks and will cover a large number of cities with multiple firms in each city. Institutional interest and commitment will be secured during this time as the company principals visit with fund managers. As the road show nears completion, the syndicate firms will know if the interest in the company is sufficient to support the offering. If a great deal of interest is expressed in the company, the offering will continue. If interest is insufficient for the needs of the syndicate and company, the offering will be "pulled" and the syndicate may rework its plan. If the interest is high, the syndicate may choose to increase the price per share of the offering to capture additional capital. Typically, if the syndicate wishes to create a "hot" offering, it will underprice the issue significantly to create a "buzz" about a company that is about to go public. Nothing will create more of a stir in the investment community than a stock that is issued at $18 per share and closes at $65 after the first day of trading. By creating the effect of a massive move on the first day of trading, everyone in the syndicate's investor pool will capture huge profits and the new stock will be the talk of Wall Street for weeks to come.

Now you've seen how a publicly traded stock evolves from the simple beginnings of excited entrepreneurs with a dream. They put in all they have, get the right management partners, find an angel, build the business, find a venture capital partner, build the business some more, find an investment banker, form an underwriting syndicate, do a dog and pony show, price the issue properly, and issue the stock. This process likely happened at some time for any common stock. For Ford stock, it happened at the beginning of the century; for Amazon.com, it happened almost yesterday. In either case, somebody somewhere started with a simple idea and followed it through thick and thin to see it to fruition.

If our children understand this process, they will gain an appreciation for how much effort goes into creating something of lasting value. As they begin to understand what it takes for ideas to become tangible companies, they will comprehend that anyone, with the right drive and determination, can make dreams come true. Once they understand that the world is at their fingertips, they will be armed with the tools necessary to create a lifetime of success, achievement, confidence, and satisfaction.

If you, as a potential investor, understand the process whereby companies become publicly traded, you will have a valuable insight to help you determine the strength of a company's foundation. Once you are comfortable with this beginning, you can make an informed and intelligent decision regarding the investment opportunity.

Besides the foundation of a company, you should evaluate several other elements before making an investment decision. The

Investor's Business Daily is an excellent publication for analyzing individual stock opportunities. In its training material, it lists seven key elements to consider when making a stock selection. The *Investor's Business Daily* calls the stock selection process the C-A-N-S-L-I-M process. We'll list the elements next.

C—Current Quarterly Earnings

A potential stock investment should show an increase in recent quarterly earnings per share (EPS) of at least 25%. The longer the increase has been maintained over previous quarters, the greater the likelihood of continued success. A minimum of five successive previous quarters should be considered. The *Investor's Business Daily* scores a company's earnings strength on a scale from 1 to 100. It is wise to invest only in companies that score greater than 90.

A—Annual Earnings

A strong company will show a growth rate in excess of 25% over a three-, four-, and five-year history. It is also helpful if the annual earnings percentage has been increasing regularly over the most recent three years.

N—New High, New Product, or New Management

By buying a stock when it is hitting a new high, you stand a good chance at being on an elevator that is going in the right direction. This is especially true when a stock breaks what is known as a resistance level. Any time a stock breaks this level, the price per share can go to substantially higher levels. Most investment professionals look for stocks that are breaking resistance levels so they and their clients can benefit from the upward movement. This increase of demand furthers the momentum of the stock's rise. You also may consider newer companies with new products and services as well as firms that have new management. How many of us wish we had bought Chrysler when Lee Iococca took over?

S—Supply and Demand, Shares Outstanding

The size of the company you invest in is important. The greater the company float (shares outstanding), the more difficult it is for the company stock to suffer a sharp downward move if a sell-off occurs. The *Investor's Business Daily* suggests looking for a company with a float of between 5 and 50 million shares outstanding. When you review a company's float, watch for a substantial increase in daily volume. Such an increase indicates that something good or something bad is about to happen. You'll be able to tell which one by the direction the stock's price is heading. If you see a stocks' price up and a trading volume percent change of 1,500%, you're probably looking at a stock that is preparing to make a move to the north because the big money is beginning to flow into the company.

L—Leaders vs. Laggards

Always buy industry leaders. The companies that continually perform well within an industry are the ones you want to own. Never buy a stock based on a "comeback because of _____" story. The chance of a percentage increase of your holdings compared to the risk you must take by buying a laggard isn't worth it. The stock's relative price strength indicates whether it is an industry leader or an industry laggard. As mentioned, the *Investor's Business Daily* lists this strength as a number between 1 and 100. It is prudent to invest only in those companies with a score above 90.

I—Institutional Sponsorship

Just as I discussed in the underwriting of a new issue of stock, institutional sponsorship is of great importance to all good listed securities. Without the sponsorship of an institution like a mutual fund or brokerage firm, a stock's volume will be relatively low and its price support will be at the mercy of the market. Institutional sponsorship enhances price stability, and other institutional investors will be more comfortable with the stock as a potential portfolio company.

M—Market Direction

All the great news in the world about a company and its performance can be offset by its market sector being down. When you decide to make a stock purchase, make sure the market is moving in the right direction and that the stock's sector is in favor overall. If both of these factors are positive, you stand a good chance at picking a good stock.

The overall methodology of the C-A-N-S-L-I-M stock selection process will help you make good stock selections. By coupling this process with your own simple observations about what a company is up to, you'll be likely to have success in your stock selection. Please notice that I said "stock selection," not "investing." The difference between the two is that if you are investing, in order to capitalize on an investment, eventually you must sell the stock to take your profits. As I have said before, the best way to achieve strong and consistent returns on your investments is to buy and hold the security.

You should be extraordinarily careful as you make your stock purchase selections. You have time to do this because your money is still in the bank with your name on it. Unfortunately, the moment you purchase a stock, something happens to your brain that makes you want to sell your shares at the drop of a hat either to capitalize on a gain or to keep from losing your shirt when the price drops slightly. If you take as long investigating why you feel like selling the stock as you took investigating why you should buy the stock, the event that caused you to ponder the decision in the first place will have gone away.

Buy and hold is the only way to create real long-term value in your portfolio. Since whatever you wind up buying is going to be with you for a while, you might as well take the time to investigate thoroughly and make a good selection.

Chapter Challenge ....

The *Investor's Business Daily* is an excellent publication for investment news and information. Its reporting and investment analysis techniques are unmatched in the investment media. This publication will provide you with invaluable insight into the financial markets and the analysis of individual securities. Pick up a copy the next time you are out and take some time going through it. Pay particular attention to the section "How to Use *SmartSelect™* Corporate Ratings." This introduction will provide you with much of the necessary data to help you improve your investment decisions. If you like to use the Internet, you can visit www.investors.com for a quick review.

....

GOAL ATTAINMENT

CHAPTER 42

Self-Esteem

Leaders are like eagles. They don't come in flocks,
they just show up every so often.

—ANONYMOUS

EVERYTHING WE HAVE DISCUSSED SO FAR RELATES TO SELF-ESTEEM. If you think about the goal attainment process, it's the effort that enhances the internal reward. By showing your children how to set a goal, understand the rules, design a course to goal attainment, work their plan, defer gratification, and attain their goal, you are providing your future leader the ultimate achievement training ground. If you help your children learn how to achieve, you teach them how to enhance their own self-esteem. The great leaders of the world have been self-motivated, self-confident, and self-sustaining.

A significant by-product to the process you have shared with your children is the pride associated with a job well done. Getting something done is one thing; doing your best to see that a job gets done right is another thing altogether. As parents, we need to make sure our children develop a commitment to do their jobs to the best of their abilities. We want to do this not because of what other people might think but because of the internal growth that occurs when a job is accomplished at the highest possible level.

We want our children to feel the personal benefits associated with a best effort. As they recognize the pleasure of these feelings, they will want to perform every task at a higher level, whether it's at school, at home, at a neighbor's, or at a friend's.

As children learn to apply themselves to the best of their abilities, they will develop pride in the process of goal attainment. Every goal that our children reach will increase their self-esteem and desire to achieve more. Once they realize the personal power that they possess, they will want to implement that power at every opportunity. The positive attitudes and excitement for life that emanate from goal attainment will be permanent and contagious. Each member of your family will grow to understand the positive impact of being empowered through goal attainment.

As children learn of their family responsibilities and accept their personal accountability for their actions within the family, they will derive natural feelings of comfort and security. These positive feelings will be enhanced by the boundaries and family customs that have been established. The family motto and family mission statement will enhance the feelings of personal belonging and individual importance to the children. The home will be a place where the children most want to be.

The environment we create within our own homes will set an example for the rest of our children's lives. Our kids can go through life excited about all the opportunity that's out there or afraid to make a move for fear of punishment. Their attitude is a result of our nurturing. If you aren't happy with the way your kids are turning out, take a look at their daily example at home and the attention they have been given. If you're excited about the way your kids are turning out, likewise, take a look at their daily example and the attention you have given them.

Remember, your children's attitudes and aptitudes are directly related to their family environment. The way your parents were with you is probably the way you are with your kids. The way you are with your kids is the way they will be with your grandchildren.

Were you treated well and encouraged to reach your highest potential, or were you disciplined and scolded into submission? Whatever the parenting technique was, you know its result because you live it daily.

Determine right now to provide the best possible environment you can for your children. Let them know of their personal power and empower them with financial intelligence. Help them to be leaders and successes in whatever they choose to do.

Chapter Challenge ....

Conduct a personal interview with yourself. Ask yourself:

Was I treated with respect by my parents?

Were the communication lines open with my parents?

Were the household rules and responsibilities made clear to me?

Was I given the chance to set and attain personal goals?

Was I given the opportunity to learn about my personal power?

Was I empowered with financial intelligence?

How have these factors affected me as an adult and as a parent?

Write your answers in either a personal journal or the family journal. Consider the same questions as they relate to you and your own children today.

....

CHAPTER 43

Raise the Bar

I am enough of an artist to draw freely upon my imagination.
Imagination is more important than knowledge. Knowledge
is limited. Imagination encircles the world.

—ALBERT EINSTEIN

AS YOU WORK WITHIN YOUR HOME AND WITH YOUR FAMILY members, you need to make sure that you are continually challenging yourselves to become better. Life provides an opportunity to test ourselves and to prove to ourselves what we are capable of. Our happiness and satisfaction are affected to the extent that we know we are doing our best.

The excitement that stems from a new challenge is what keeps us sharp, excited, and motivated. We should share this sensation with our children. They have as much a need to be challenged as we do, but they will derive greater benefit because of their stage in life. If we continually offer our children the opportunity to advance to a higher level of accomplishment, we provide them with the basic building blocks for success and happiness.

Learning is a process that evolves from attaining basic intelligence a bit at a time and then going on to master more sophisticated concepts. You need to keep this in mind when you work with your children. Start small and work up from there. If you start with something too challenging, you run the risk of discouragement. If you fail to stimulate, you run the risk of allowing complacency to set in. These same statements apply to our own lives as well. We need to be careful not to try to tackle too much at first; at the same time, we must keep ourselves motivated by new challenges.

As children build their self-esteem through accumulated achievements, you need to monitor their progress carefully. Personal success is important. As those successes build up on one another, children will gain a significant amount of confidence. It's this self-confidence that will enable them to choose to embark on their own adventure away from home and possibly away from a conventional employment decision. Those achievers who use their imagination to create new and better ways of doing things are the movers and shakers of the next generation. They will be empowered by a high level of self-confidence, which emanates from personal success. This personal success will be accumulated through accomplishment within the home. As parents, we provide the opportunity for that accomplishment.

As children grow and mature through the various stages of development, we will see them take on new and exciting challenges for themselves. We will do the best we can to make sure they have all the resources necessary to conquer those challenges. Eventually our children will pack their belongings and move out of our homes and into a life of their own. Their preparation for that event starts with our teaching them the real-world financial skills they will need.

Our children's progression within our homes should culminate with the ability to sustain themselves in a life of their own. The path from their first goal and their first opportunity to self-sustenance is a long and complicated one. Along the way there surely will be rough spots and smooth spots, high peaks and low valleys. The journey will be filled with as many different challenges, obstacles, accomplishments, and victories as you can think of. Even though the road is long, the path can be clearly marked with a well-conceived action plan that you will provide.

Walking along the path as a family, you will all experience the journey together. At times some of you will notice the rain that pelts your face while the others notice a rainbow in the distance. Some will complain about how steep the hill is while others contemplate the long coast downhill. Each of you will have a different frame of reference for the same experience, and you won't always agree on which course of action to take. But as long as you stick together and support one another throughout the journey, your memories will be pleasant, the financial future will be bright, and each step you take will be on higher ground than the previous one.

Chapter Challenge ....

At your next family night, have all family members write a story about who they are and what they think about themselves. Have them write down what they think other family members think about them. Then have them write a story about what is going to happen to them in the future. Let them know that these stories can be private if they want them to be. After everyone writes down a story, seal them in an envelope and mark on it "NOT TO BE OPENED UNTIL _____." Enter a date twenty years from that date. Place the envelope in a safe location, such as a safe-deposit box, and forget about it for a while. Then get busy working with the kids on their next goal.

CHAPTER 44

....

Help Somebody
Else

*The true measure of a man is how he treats someone
who can do him absolutely no good.*

—ANN LANDERS

IN THIS BOOK YOU'VE SPENT A GREAT DEAL OF TIME ESTABLISHING
personal goals, defining responsibilities, earning money, and
accomplishing objectives. The children are probably quite positive
about their progress, and we, as parents, are feeling pretty good
about what terrific examples we have become. But even after all of
this progress and positive experience, we've still not talked about
one of our greatest sources of personal happiness and gratification
in life: helping those less fortunate than ourselves.

As our children set goals and begin to earn an income, we should
make sure that a portion of that income is allocated to some sort
of external contribution. This amount can be at your discretion
but shouldn't be more than 10 or 15% of what they earn. It should
be calculated weekly and deducted from their checkbook register
the same day the deposit entry is made. It's important for them
to understand that there are contributions that we make and

responsibilities that we pay for that are natural parts of life's earning process. These funds that are deducted could be offered to your local church or synagogue, a homeless shelter, or any other worthy charitable organization.

A great deal of happiness and personal satisfaction can come from giving aid to those in need. The experience we gain and the example we set by donating time and resources back to our community can be a tremendous source of emotional gratification. Our children need to be shown an example that they can emulate as well as be given the opportunity to grow emotionally.

Some of the things that we can do within our homes to promote a feeling of contribution are as easy as being mindful of the needs of others in the house. If we continually promote an attitude of contribution among family members, each person will benefit from the positive environment that is established. Likewise, if we instill a sense of community service within our family, each member will grow and mature expecting that community service is a natural part of a quality life.

As a family, we have a real responsibility to our eldest members, our grandparents. My grandmother, in her later years, had a very nice apartment in a wonderful retirement community in Grand Rapids, Michigan. She had many friends and many activities to keep her busy. In fact, at times her schedule was as busy as mine as an up-and-coming stockbroker. But even though she had many activities and many friends and her schedule was always full, there was no substitute for when family members would go to see her. My cousins and I would drop in to say hello when we were in the area, and we would bring her great-grandchildren along as often as possible.

Nothing would light up her face more than my wife and I and our three boys cramming through her door to drop in for a visit. Often the stop was out of the way, and many times there were other things that needed to get done, but visiting meant so much to my grandma that we never missed an opportunity. My cousins were the same way, and Grandma always had somebody dropping in to say hello or drop off something sweet to eat. Donna Kennedy Stawski was one loved and often-visited grandma.

Unfortunately, I can't say the same for some of the other residents of her facility. Many elderly residents had family in town who rarely dropped in to visit. When we walked down the hallway, Jordan and Jacob (Preston was being carried at the time) would get stopped half a dozen times each way by lonely grandparents just wanting a bit of attention from a child. It broke my heart to know that these forgotten people had wonderful stories to tell about an incredible life but had no one dropping by to tell them to.

If you have living grandparents in your family, please spend time with them. Let your children know how important it is not to forget our heritage and to glean as much information as we can from the older generation.

The elderly who are living today have experienced the most technological change of any generation that has ever occupied this planet. The generation that is passing now remembers when the automobile didn't exist. They recall most of the great technological advances of the past century. The insight and information that these incredible people possess are invaluable to a generation that is growing up without a significant challenge or adversity.

Other opportunities for your family to learn about helping others may come in the form of donating time at a local shelter or mission. Nothing will help your children appreciate what they have more than visiting and serving at one of these charitable locations. Your church or synagogue may be able to help you find other opportunities for your family to serve.

Chapter Challenge ....

If you have elderly grandparents or great-grandparents, make sure you visit them within the next week or two. If they live out of town, make sure you call them during the next week and give your children an opportunity to talk with them at length. Have the kids ask about what it was like when they were the same age as the children and if they remember any funny or interesting stories. If so, listen in on the conversation, and write the story or stories in your family journal.

. . . .

ATTAIN AGAIN

CHAPTER 45

Your Greatest Opportunity

I must study War and Politics, so my children may
study Science and Engineering, so their children
may study Literature and Music.

—JOHN ADAMS

WHAT IS THE PURPOSE OF LIFE? WHY ARE WE HERE? WHERE WILL my greatest happiness come from? These three major questions have been stumping people for ages. Are we here to gain as much wealth as quickly as we can? Should we attempt to accumulate as many toys as we can to impress the socks off of all our friends while we're here? Maybe we need to dedicate our lives to showing other people what great contributors we are and how popular we can be. It could be that our personal satisfaction will come from having the nicest yard and most beautiful home on our street, or maybe by having the nicest car. Surely material wealth is the key to personal happiness and satisfaction.

Take a look around. Really, take a look around and observe what you see. Look at the faces of the people intent on conquering the world. Look at the expressions of the driven, dedicated fortune-builders. What expression do you see? Is it joy? Is it peace? Is it happiness? Or is it stress? If fortune-builders haven't balanced their family and children in the equation, it's probably stress.

Can you pick out the key word in the last paragraph, the one word that brings things into focus and enables us all to enjoy life to its fullest? It's the word "balanced." We all need to have balance in our lives. It's important for us to provide for our families the best we can, and it's important for us to be dedicated to our careers. At the same time we must give our families our best and be dedicated to nurturing the next generation. Our spouses must be at the center of our attention and should clearly recognize the great impact they have on our lives. In the entire world, no one will ever be as important to you as your spouse. If you don't believe it, think about who was with you during the hard times and who will be with you when you're old and wrinkly. In this crazy world of rapid-fire change, who is the one person in your life that doesn't change? It's your spouse, and you need to let them know clearly where they stand in your life. We always must strive to do our best at whatever it is that we are doing, including being a mom or a dad or a son or a daughter or a husband or a wife or a friend.

Think back to when you were most happy, to a time when you smiled and laughed the most. Think back to when things were less complicated than they are today. I'll bet it was a time when you had balance. You may have been working harder, studying harder, and starting a new family all at the same time, but you had balance.

For me, this time of happiness was when I lived in South Carolina, stationed at Shaw Air Force Base. I was enlisted, working from 0700 to 1600 (that's 7:00 A.M. to 4:00 P.M. for you regular folks), going home to change clothes, see my family, and grab a bite to eat, heading to class at 5:15 and staying there until 10:20 P.M., Monday through Thursday. Friday, Saturday, and Sunday included a bit of homework, but we did stuff as a family then. We went to Columbia to the mall, we went to Myrtle Beach to swim, we went to Charleston to see the historic sites, we spent quality time together. It was the balance of dedicated hard work and study with quality family time that created the happiness we had.

The balance of family and hard work is a winning combination for everyone. By applying yourself to the best of your abilities in your career, you will see the greatest emotional gratification and financial reward. By clearly defining your work commitment time and your family time, you will lay the foundation for a solid family experience and great relationships will develop.

This book is about financial intelligence. We've spent a great deal of time teaching our children how to set goals, earn, save, be responsible, defer gratification, and achieve goals. But what is the real financial intelligence gained here? It is the ability to identify how much is enough to meet the needs of our families and then take the rest of the time to build relationships with our family members.

The processes we have been working on together have been designed to help you teach your children basic money management skills. But more important, they have been designed to help you interact with your children at a higher level. The lessons taught how to communicate more effectively and build a family team. By now you have had the opportunity to interact with your family members in such a way that you'll be able to build on those relationships. Through your family and personal journals you'll be able to keep track of what's going on in your home. Through your family night you'll learn and have fun together. By maintaining a goal reminder sheet and an allowance calculator, you'll make sure that everybody always has a goal and is applying him- or herself to goal attainment. The communication levels should be high, and family interaction should be supported at a maximum level.

So, let me ask you again: What is the purpose of life? Why are we here? Where will our greatest happiness come from? If you truly have financial intelligence, you will know the answers to these questions.

Chapter Challenge ....

Ponder the three questions asked at the beginning of this
chapter and write detailed answers in your personal journal.
The more details you can think of, the greater the benefit
you will derive. At your next family night, pose the questions
to your family members and share your responses with
them. Have your family members think about the questions
and formulate their own answers for the family journal.
Make sure you continue to use the charts provided throughout this book. Nothing will help your family stay on track
more than consistent nurturing provided by the parent.

....

CHAPTER 46

··

Happiness

Dedication and Responsibility, far beyond the laws
that govern man, releases the power within you,
to attain the wisdom of the universe.

—CHRISTINE LANE

WE'VE COME A LONG WAY TOGETHER OVER THE LAST SEVERAL WEEKS. Your ability to communicate and work with your family team has increased. It's hoped that your family has become more united and is interacting at a much higher level than ever before. The principles outlined in this book have evolved over the years in my family, and I hope they have been of significant benefit to yours.

Now it is helpful to review some of the key points and ideas discussed in this book. We've covered a lot of ground, and it is good to take a moment for review.

When you first started this book, you needed to set the financial intelligence stage for your family and create a home environment that was conducive to the lessons that were going to be taught. In order to accomplish this, you needed to take a close look at yourself and examine what kind of example you have been to your children. You made sure that your family felt like a family team through the family motto, a family mission statement, and a family journal. You took a close look at your family's financial habits

and set the stage preparatory to teaching your children basic
financial principles.

Once the communication levels were open and functioning,
when family trust was established and everyone was prepared to
interact at a higher level, you learned the rules of the game. Just as
any other activity in life, if there are rules involved, people need to
know them before stepping in. A team would never go onto the
playing field hoping to win a game if they didn't know, in great
detail, the specific rules of their game. Likewise, in an environment as interactive and dynamic as a family, all the rules need to
be disclosed and posted for all the players to see and understand.

As family team members got a grip on the rules of the game,
they were prepared to learn the first step toward accomplishment
and personal achievement, goal setting. Just as in a family trip
across the country, if you don't know where you are or where
you're going, you might as well not even turn on the ignition. By
setting the rules, the family knows where it is. By setting the goal,
family members know where they want to be. By posting a picture
of their desired destination (the goal), they are continually
reminded of their objective and can stay motivated.

At this stage, kids know where they are, where they want to be,
and the rules of the game; now they are ready for opportunity. By
giving them the opportunity to help out around the house, you
provide the vehicle that will transport them to their goal destination. Opportunity jobs enable children to take control of their
environment. How determined they are to attain their goal is the
only limit on how quickly they can reach their objective. The
greater the number and variety of opportunities available, the
greater children's flexibility and freedom to attain their objectives.

Family emotions sometimes can run a little hot and things can
get out of control, if we let them. For this reason, everyone knows
the household rules ahead of time, and have the rules posted where
we all can see them. By predetermining the consequences to the
family rules, we as parents can effectively take the negative emo-

tions out of parenting. By ensuring that the communication levels remain high through the practiced interaction of a regular family night, we reduce the likelihood of an unexpected emotional outburst.

Some of the written records maintained within the family are a family journal for public family-related ideas and personal journals for private and personal matters. These written records are helpful to the family and the individual in providing an outlet for expressing feelings. They also provide a mechanism to record the family history that will be cherished in years to come as the family environment changes and evolves.

A more specific written record that is kept, related to earnings education, is the allowance calculator. This weekly record provides family members with an opportunity to record earnings and responsibilities as they occur during the week. The combination of the allowance calculator and the goal reminder sheet provides the goal destination transport vehicle whereby children can attain their goals. A personal checkbook can be maintained to keep track of where the money comes from and where it goes throughout the course of goal attainment. The checkbook provides children with their first exposure to personal budgeting and the importance of accounting for each dollar that is earned.

As parents, we too need to establish personal financial guidelines and budgets. By taking control of our finances, we not only lessen the stress on ourselves but we also set the positive example for those living in our homes. Personal financial record keeping is one of the greatest responsibilities we have as the leaders of our family.

By knowing and understanding our personal financial situation, we position ourselves to manage financial resources proactively. By having an active personal financial plan, we set the stage for ultimate financial success in life. Within this financial plan, we manage debt, structure saving and investment, and complete the image of our overall financial life-scape.

If we as parents have a proactive plan for financial goal attainment, and if our children are given the opportunity to do the same, we position ourselves to enjoy the self-esteem, self-confidence, and pride that accompanies personal achievement. This achievement combined with positive family communication skills will do more to enhance family relationships than anything else we can do.

The ultimate objective of creating financial intelligence is to gain an understanding of personal happiness and satisfaction with life. We are not interested in accumulating the largest number of toys or having the biggest and nicest home, we are interested in knowing how best to contribute to our family and society. This contribution, which includes a determined effort to be the best, will do more for our personal happiness than any material possession ever could. By taking a genuine pride in the process of life, we earn the reward of quality family relationships and true personal happiness.

> *Yesterday is a canceled check;*
> *Tomorrow is a promissory note;*
> *Today is the only cash you have;*
> *So spend it wisely.*
>
> —KAY LYONS

Appendix

Every generation gets their chance,
the Internet is ours.

Markus Eberli

The Internet provides literally a world of resources to your home through your personal computer. If you don't have access to this amazing tool, I highly suggest you find a way to make it happen. A number of Internet-based computer deals are available where you can get a computer for free if you agree to an Internet service up front. Ordinarily it is wise not to incur additional monthly obligations, but in the case of Internet access, I would bend the rules a bit. The benefits derived from Internet access, if properly applied, will far outweigh the monthly access fee.

A list of some of the sites that may be helpful to you and your children follows. These sites will provide you with a wealth of information and will be beneficial to your family as you implement the principles outlined in this book. If you are a first-time Internet user, your ability to navigate the Web effectively will be enhanced by visiting, learning, and revisiting these educational and motivational resources. Good luck.

Cash University
www.cashuniversity.com

Your access to financial literacy materials and ideas for your family.

Family Search
www.familysearch.org

A great site for genealogical research to define and enhance the strength of your family roots.

Financial Peace
www.financialpeace.com

Commonsense financial information from Dave Ramsey on his three-hour radio progam, live, 1:00 to 4:00 P.M. CST. Tune in online today.

Franklin Covey
www.franklincovey.com

World leader in day planning products that provide tools for effective living. Dedicated to helping you move in the right direction by focusing your efforts on what matters most to you.

Jump$tart Coalition
www.jumpstartcoalition.org

Financial Smarts for Students. Curriculum enrichment materials to ensure that basic personal financial management skills are attained during the K–12 educational experience.

Junior Achievement
www.ja.org

Since 1919, Junior Achievement has made an impact on young people by educating and inspiring them to value free enterprise, business, and economics to improve the quality of their lives.

Kids, Parents, and Money
www.kidsparentsandmoney.com
The place for information, printable forms, and links to other money sites for kids.

KidsBank.com
www.kidsbank.com
A fun place for children to learn about money and banking brought to you by Sovereign Bank.

Nightingale Conant
www.nightingale.com
Personal and business resources for greater effectiveness. Products, services, online audio clips, speakers, and seminars for self-improvement.

PCQuote.com
www.pcquote.com
A great resource for personal financial investment information. Includes Quote Tools, Markets-at-a-Glance, Research, Breaking News, and Points of Interest on Stocks, Options, Futures, Brokers, Shopping, and Products. Super financial site.

PocketCard
www.pocketcard.com
PocketCard is a new, high-tech, Visa card available as one of the most powerful tools ever developed to teach financial responsibility. Kids will be free to make purchases both on- and offline, while parents maintain control over spending limits.

RocketCash
www.rocketcash.com
Kids can buy cool stuff online without their parent's credit card. RocketCash is the kid's ewallet that gives you the license to shop online.

Sage Scholars
www.student-aid.com

Their College Insight Tuition Rewards Program is a visionary approach to saving for college education. The program will encourage you to plan and save for your children's undergraduate college education and reward you for doing so. Log on to see how.

The Stock Market Game
www.smg2000.org

This site is the premier educational program that stimulates learning about economics, finance, and the American economic system. This exciting real-world simulation enables participants to discover the risks and rewards involved in decision making, the sources and uses of capital, and other related economic concepts.

Young Investors Network
www.smithbarney.com/yin

Kids can learn how to take control of their future and get what they want out of life. They will gain the knowledge they need to get a huge head start in building their dreams. They can set goals and design a personalized plan to accumulate the money they will need to get there.

Glossary

Allowance Calculator—A job chart designed to track job accomplishment and responsibility behaviors throughout the week. By adding the amounts earned through job accomplishment and subtracting any consequence items, a net weekly allowance is determined.

Angel—That heavenly investor who invests seed money into a fledgling organization to give it the capital it needs to develop into a bona fide entity. Angel investment is the first step for a company in the corporate growth process prior to a venture capital investment. Without angel investors, many of today's publicly traded companies wouldn't be around.

C-A-N-S-L-I-M—A popular investment selection system focusing on seven select financial and market indicators. The C-A-N-S-L-I-M process helps potential investors in common stock determine which ones have the greatest potential for growth. The seven indicators are: (1) current quarterly earnings growth; (2) annual earnings growth; (3) new price high, product or management; (4) supply and demand, shares outstanding; (5) leaders vs. laggards; (6) institutional sponsorship; and (7) market direction.

Collateral—Used in conjunction with the family borrowing contract, the collateral represents the item being family-financed. The item that is purchased will be recognized as collateral for the borrowing contract and will be attached to the note for as long as it takes the borrower to pay off the note. By helping your children understand the principle of collateral, you'll motivate them to honor their note and perhaps even pay it off early.

Communication Enhancers—Those documents and habits that are established within the home to foster personal relationships and communication. Examples of these include a family mission statement, family journal, and family night.

Debt Buster—The process of eliminating personal debt through a structured plan. Typically it is recommended to work from the smallest to the largest debt over a period of time. A commitment not to incur additional debt is necessary for effective debt busting.

Default—You'll want to go over this term with your children at the beginning of any borrowing exercise. Your children need to know that they have entered a serious agreement with you as the parent-lender. Your children should understand that if they do not honor the agreement, there will be serious implications, namely, the repossession of their collateral until the note is remedied.

Dow Jones Industrial Average—A widely tracked market index that is used to measure the activity and direction of the overall market. The DJIA is an average assessment of the market as a whole consisting of thirty select, large industrial companies. The index components, which differ over time, represent approximately 20% of the market value of all New York Stock Exchange stocks.

Down Payment—Used in conjunction with the family borrowing contract, the down payment simply represents the amount of money your young borrower must come up with in order to qualify for extension of family credit. The down payment could be as high as 50% or as low as 10%, depending on your family standards and the amount of the item being family-financed.

Earnings Evolution—The process of earning through more sophisticated tasks as the child grows. Beginning in the kitchen at home (feed pets, set table) and evolving to other people's money (mow neighbor's yard, lemonade stand), this evolution moves the individual gradually into a real-world environment through practical experience.

Emergency Fund—A family cash account that contains the equivalent of one or more months of expenses. This fund establishes the most basic level of financial security for the family.

Family Com-tract—A document created by family members to clarify household rules and responsibilities. This contract serves to define individual boundaries and expectations and eliminate any questions that may exist about an individual's role in the family.

Family Goal Fund—A savings account set aside for the accumulation of monies needed to attain a family objective. This objective offers family members the opportunity to work together toward a common goal of a vacation, watercraft, or something as simple as a weekend away.

Family Jobs—Those tasks around the home that are done by children as personal responsibility jobs. These tasks typically are related to personal hygiene (make bed, clean room) and are expected in exchange for the food, clothing, and shelter provided by family membership.

Family Journal—A document maintained by family members to record significant and not-so-significant events that occur throughout the ordinary course of the day. This communication vehicle and record enables family members to share a degree of free expression and thought about the events that occur within the family experience.

Family Mission Statement—This document serves as the family constitution in order to define the family's most basic values and objectives. Most important family decisions can be clarified and influenced by referring to the family mission statement during the decision process.

Family Motto—An easily remembered phrase or slogan that captures the essence of your unique family experience. The family motto serves as an immediate reminder to family members that will clarify the special nature of their family team.

Family Night—An evening set aside every week to review family issues and to be together. This night is special and necessary to the development of communication and relationships within the family.

Family Team—A phrase that identifies the special relationship that exists among family members. By identifying your family members as team members, a feeling of unity and a common objective can be fostered easily.

Family Time Capsule—A dated record of statements regarding the family environment, relationships, goals, objectives, and circumstances. The packet is to be sealed and marked with a do-not-open-until date and then stored in a secure location.

Financial Intelligence—The state of financial awareness that is necessary to accomplish lifetime objectives and ultimate financial success. Financial intelligence enables the individual to break out of an immediate gratification mind-set in favor of a more meaningful and long-lasting, forward-thinking intelligence.

Financial Rudderlessness—The state in which individuals with no financial direction or objective in their lives exist. This state is brought on by a lack of basic financial intelligence. "Living from paycheck to paycheck" is a symptom of financial rudderlessness.

Gimmes—A mental state that exists in most children and a small percentage of adults that causes an uncontrollable desire to be gratified immediately by the purchase of an otherwise unnecessary item while shopping.

Goal Attainment Process (GAP)—The fundamental cycle of financial achievement throughout one's life. The process consists of setting an objective, looking for opportunity, working to earn, budgeting, saving, deferring gratification, and attaining the goal.

Goal Reminder Sheet—A visual reminder of the goal one has set. This document, placed in a frequently visited location, usually consists of a picture of the goal item, its price, and an anticipated attainment date.

Initial Public Offering—The introduction of a company's stock into the public market through one of the stock exchanges. An investment banking house typically forms a syndicate of several firms to introduce the security to the market and support its price initially.

After the market price becomes stabilized, banker support will be reduced until the stock freely trades based on its own merits and investor demand.

Kiddie Casino—A term used to describe anyplace where money is revalued into tickets or tokens. These tickets or tokens are then spent on games of chance to win prizes worth significantly less than the dollars spent participating in the games.

Learntrepreneur—The state of children as they begin to understand the benefits of relying on themselves to create an income. Becoming aware that they can determine their own opportunity (lemonade stand) instead of having to rely on a parent to supply an opportunity to earn (clean garage for $5).

Mail Money—The income derived from activities and investment outside of your primary source of income. This could include rental property income, stock dividends, interest on loans made, and multilevel marketing activities.

Mini-Money Lesson—The experience of enabling a child to pick out an item from the store, usually a "gimme" item, set it as an objective, accomplish a task for the parent, be paid for the effort, and then be brought back to the store to purchase the item. These events usually transpire over only a few hours in order to make the event an immediate and lasting one for the child.

The Nasdaq Composite Index—A measure of all Nasdaq common stocks listed on the Nasdaq stock system. This composite includes over 5,000 companies and is one of the most widely followed and quoted major market indexes.

Opportunity Jobs—Those tasks around the home, ordinarily accomplished by the parent, offered to children as an opportunity to earn. By assisting the parent—lessening his or her workload—the children earn compensation for their effort.

Other People's Money (OPM)—To work outside of the home for compensation. It is more challenging, fun, and profitable to work for other people's money than within the home. OPM is the basis for the most mature stages of the earnings evolution.

Over the Counter—A term used to describe a stock that is traded via the National Association of Securities Dealers Automated Quotron (Nasdaq) system. This system allows broker/dealers to trade directly with one another over the wire without the need of a physical location for the trade to take place. Until the advent of the Internet, over-the-counter stocks were traditionally smaller and less actively traded, geographically limited issues. New Internet companies have changed the Nasdaq dynamics in that these companies can grow to massive market capitalization over a relatively short period of time.

Parental Harassment Techniques—The attention-getting techniques implemented by children when they are not given the attention they feel they need. These techniques can vary from asking "but why" to full-blown temper tantrums.

Quality Scale—An opportunity job scale that establishes the requirements for a job well done. A job done halfway earns only half or less of the posted compensation. Earners will quickly understand the importance of conscientious effort in task accomplishment when job expectations are clearly defined.

Registered Exchange—A term used to define a stock exchange that trades one of the over 4,000 listed stocks. Listing requirements are rigorous, and only the largest and most stable companies will qualify for a new listing. The most notable of the registered exchanges are the New York Stock Exchange and the American Stock Exchange.

Repossess—As part of your explanation of default on a note, you'll want to explain that repossession of their collateral will be necessary until they can pay off the note in its entirety. This is necessary in order for your children to grasp the significance of their decision not to keep up the payments on the note agreement.

Title—When dealing with children, it is important to help them understand as many financial terms and principles as possible. In this case, the term "title" simply refers to the recipient of the item purchased under a family borrowing contract. The title to their item will be given to them upon note completion. You can help them maintain an entire file on the loan by keeping the note contract, the down payment check, all payment checks, any earning records, and finally their released title when the note is satisfied.

Venture Capital—Investment funds that are made available to worthy, early-stage companies for business and market development. These funds are usually managed by a team of business leaders and have strict criteria for investment. These funds usually come from affluent families or large corporate pools of money. Venture capital investments usually range from $500,000 (only a few) to $50,000,000 and higher. In times of economic prosperity, minimum investment amounts rise because the supply of money available and the number of qualified deals both grow. A venture capital firm will spend as much time investigating a $1 million dollar deal as they will a $50 million deal. The percentage return is likely to be the same, so the smaller deals don't get funded.

Index

Note: Page numbers followed by *fig.* indicate figures. Those followed by *g* indicate glossary items.

Visit:

www.kidsparentsandmoney.com

···

The online resource for readers of Bill Stawski's
Kids, Parents & Money

There you will find:

- over 20 printable forms used in the book
- useful parenting resources
- PocketCard—The U.S. debit card for kids
- premium links for kids, parents, and money

www.kidsparentsandmoney.com

···

NEW

CASH UNIVERSITY
Money Management Kit For Kids

Parents Choice Gold Award

This unique and innovative learning system teaches kids to:

• Set their own goals
• Save money
• Earn rewards
• Achieve success
• Plan and budget for expenditures
• Use a checkbook
• Be a responsible & helpful member of the family

To order call toll free 800.209.4800
Cash University at www.cashuniversity.com

Kids will "Learn to Earn" and be financially responsible

...with this comprehensive money management system designed by a financial expert for his own children. Kit includes: instructors' manual and audio cassette, goal reminder sheet, allowance calculator, college savings board, family fun coupon book, children's checkbook and course correspondence.

#8107 $24.95